STRANGER
IN THE
VALLEY
OF THE
KINGS

STRANGER
IN THE
VALLEY
OF THE
KINGS

Solving the Mystery of an Ancient Egyptian Mummy

AHMED OSMAN

1817

HARPER & ROW, PUBLISHERS, SAN FRANCISCO

Cambridge, Hagerstown, New York, Philadelphia, Washington
London, Mexico City, São Paulo, Singapore, Sydney

FIRST U.S. EDITION

Library of Congress Cataloging-in-Publication Data

Osman, Ahmed, 1934–
  Stranger in the Valley of the Kings.

Bibliography: p.
  Includes index.
  1. Egypt—History—To 332 B.C. 2. Joseph (Son of Jacob) 3. Yuya.
4. Mummies—Egypt. I. Title.
DT87.085   1988   932   88-45152
ISBN 0-06-250674-9

88 89 90 91 92 RRD 10 9 8 7 6 5 4 3 2 1

PUBLISHER'S NOTE

More than twenty years of dedicated research and study have gone into the making of this book. In writing it, the author's chief concern initially was to assemble a mass of complex evidence designed to convince biblical experts and qualified Egyptologists that some of the accepted beliefs about the ancient links between the tribe of Israel and the Egypt of the Pharaohs were ill-founded.

We felt, however, that his theories were not only bound to prove controversial, but deserved, and would be appreciated by, a far wider audience. The book is therefore published in two sections. The first, largely uninterrupted by references to sources and footnotes, is a straightforward account of the author's attempt to establish that an intuition, which came to him one winter's night as he sat reading the Old Testament by the fire, was more than fanciful imagining: the second contains most of the source material and notes as well as some of the scholarship that, while absorbing to experts, seemed likely to prove somewhat abstruse for the general reader.

ACKNOWLEDGEMENTS

The author would like to thank the following for permission to quote from copyright material:

The Committee of the Egypt Exploration Society for quotations from Alan Gardiner's article 'A New Rendering of Egyptian Texts', published in *The Journal of Egyptian Archaeology*, Vol. 5, 1918, and from the report of Henri Naville to the first Annual General Meeting of the Society in 1884; Oxford University Press for quotations from *Egypt of the Pharaohs* by Alan Gardiner (1961) and from *The Language of the Pentateuch in its Relation to Egyptian* by A. S. Yahuda (1933); Ta-Ha Publishers Limited for quotations from the English translation of the Koran by A. Yusuf Ali; E. J. Brill for quotations from *A Study of the Biblical Story of Joseph* by Donald B. Redford (1970); the Director of Cairo Museum for quotations from the report by Grafton Eliot Smith published in the *Catalogue général des antiquités égyptiennes du Musée du Caire* (1908); Yale University Press for quotations from *The Hyksos* by John van Seters (1966); Doubleday & Co., Inc. for quotations from *The World of the Old Testament* by Cyrus H. Gordon (1958); Peter Smith Publishers (Gloucester, MA) for quotations from *The Archaeology of Palestine* by William Foxwell Albright; the Egyptian Organisation of Antiquity for quotations from *Slavery in Pharaonic Egypt* by Abd el-Mohsen Bakir, supplement to *Annales du service des antiquités de l'Egypte*, Vol. 18, 1952; the American Research Centre in Egypt for quotations from an article by A. R. Schulman published in their *Journal*, Vol. 2, 1963; Mr K. A. Kitchen for quotations from his book *Ancient Orient and the Old Testament* published by Intervarsity Press, Illinois (1966).

Extracts from the Authorised King James Version of the Bible, which is Crown Copyright in the United Kingdom, are reproduced by permission of Eyre & Spottiswoode (Publishers) Limited, Her Majesty's Printers, London.

The author is deeply indebted to the Director of Cairo Museum for most of the photographs reproduced in this book. The photographs showing the head of Amenhotep III from Thebes and the bust of Ramses II removed from Thebes by Belzoni, are reproduced by Courtesy of the Trustees of the British Museum; the photograph of the statue of Anen is reproduced by permission of the Superintendent of the Museo Egizio, Turin; the bas-relief of Sitamun is reproduced Courtesy of the Petrie Museum, University College London (IC.14373); the photographs of Sitamun's kohl-tube is from the Carnarvon Collection, gift of Edward S. Harkness, 1926 (26.7.910), the head of Tutankhamun from the Rogers Fund, 1950 (23.10.1), and the statue of Horemheb from Memphis, a gift of Mr and Mrs V. Everit Macy, 1923 (50.6), and are reproduced Courtesy of the Trustees of the Metropolitan Mueum of Art, New York.

There are no words adequate to express the author's gratitude to Mr H. J. Weaver for his help in preparing the manuscript for publication. He would also like to give Miss Tessa Harrow his special thanks, for without her keen interest and wide knowledge of the subject, this book would not have come to light.

A. O.

CONTENTS

Publisher's Note   5
Acknowledgements   7
List of Illustrations   11
Introduction   13

BOOK ONE: A FATHER TO PHARAOH
1   The Tomb of Yuya   21
2   Voices from the Past   29
3   A Special Family   33
4   A Special Son   44
5   Joseph in the Koran   54
6   The Time of Yuya   62
7   Kings from the Desert   69
8   Chariots of War . . . or Peace?   75
9   The Egypt of Joseph   84
10 The Lost Cities   100
11 Sojourn   114
12 Doppelgänger   120
13 Death of the Gods   137

BOOK TWO: NOTES AND SOURCES
1   Abraham's Victim   145
2   Biblical Sources   153
3   Who Was Tuya?   160
4   Joseph's Name   161

Bibliography   164
Index   167

LIST OF ILLUSTRATIONS

BLACK AND WHITE PHOTOGRAPHS

Between pages 32 and 33
The Tomb of Yuya in the Valley of the Kings
Yuya's sarcophagus
The sarcophagus of Yuya's wife, Tuya
Yuya's third, innermost coffin
Tuya's inner coffin
Details of the upper parts of Tuya's outer and inner coffins
Tuya's golden mask
Yuya's mummy
Frontal and profile views of Yuya's mummy
Two views of Tuya's mummy

Between pages 64 and 65
Canopic boxes of Yuya and Tuya
Canopic jar with mummified liver
Painted wooden boxes belonging to Yuya
Yuya's necklace of gold and lapis lazuli
Papyrus and leather sandals from the tomb
Bed with panelled headpiece found in the tomb
Tuthmosis III, from Karnak
Chapter 110 from *The Book of the Dead*, from the long papyrus
    found in Yuya's tomb
Chapters 148 and 151 from *The Book of the Dead*, showing the
    seven celestial cows
Tuthmosis IV and his mother Tia, from Karnak
The Dream Stele of Tuthmosis IV
Colossi of Amenhotep III and his wife Tiye, from Thebes
The head of Amenhotep III, from Thebes
The head of Queen Tiye, found by Petrie in Sinai

Between pages 96 and 97
Coffer from the tomb of Yuya, adorned with the names of
    Amenhotep III and Tiye
Alabaster vase from Yuya's tomb, with the names of Amenhotep III
    and Tiye
Front and back views of Sitamun's smallest chair from Yuya's tomb
Sitamun's second chair
The largest chair, decorated with scenes showing Sitamun
Sitamun's kohl-tube of bright blue faience, found at Thebes
Bas-relief of Sitamun, found by Petrie in the Temple of Amenhotep II
Chariot found in Yuya's tomb
Ramses II, found at Thebes
Colossus of Ramses II, found at Tanis
The Israel Stele of Merenptah, discovered by Petrie at Thebes
Detail of the stele, showing the name of Israel

Between pages 128 and 129
Brick 'store chambers' discovered by Naville at Tell el-Maskhuta
Seti I and his son Prince Ramses, from the Temple of Abydos
Asiatic and negro prisoners, from the tomb of Horemheb
Horemheb as a scribe, before he seized the throne
Aye, thought to be Yuya's son, and his wife Tey, from Amarna
Anen, brother of Queen Tiye and Yuya's elder son
Yuya facing Osiris, from *The Book of the Dead*
Amenhotep, son of Habu, a magician of Yuya's time, found at
    Karnak
Amenhotep IV (Akhnaten) from the Aten temple at Karnak
Stele showing Akhnaten, Nefertiti and three of their daughters
Upper part of an altar showing Akhnaten, Nefertiti and their
    daughter Merytaten, found at Tell el-Amarna
Three representations of Tutankhamun

MAPS   *page*

Western Asia in the Amarna Age   40
Egypt   72
The Eastern Delta   104

INTRODUCTION

Conventional accounts of the life of Joseph, the Hebrew patriarch who took the tribe of Israel down to Egypt, are in many respects unsatisfactory. We are told of strange prophecies and dramatic events, but they are not on the whole linked together in any logical framework of cause and effect; we read of bizarre behaviour, but are left largely in the dark about why the characters concerned behaved as they did; we are assured by scholars that these stirring events took place at one point in history when there is abundant evidence, both in the Bible and elsewhere, that they took place at an entirely different time.

To summarise Joseph's personal story briefly at this stage, his own links with the Egypt of the Pharaohs are said to have begun when he was sold into slavery by his jealous half-brothers at the age of seventeen. Despite this inauspicious start, he rose in time to the exalted rank of vizier, the virtual ruler of Egypt under the king, and eventually sent for all his family—the tribe of Israel—to join him. These events are generally held to have taken place early in the reign of the Hyksos kings, Asiatic shepherds with some Semitic, Amurrite and other elements among them, who invaded Egypt around 1659 BC and ruled for more than a century. Joseph later died in Egypt, after foretelling the Exodus and extracting a promise that his bones would one day be re-buried in his homeland. The tribe of Israel are said to have remained in Egypt for four hundred and thirty years until they fell under Egyptian oppression, whereupon Moses led the Exodus to the Promised Land, taking the bones of Joseph with him for re-burial. Most modern scholars place the time of the Exodus at around 1200 BC, towards the end of the long reign of Ramses II, the third king of the Nineteenth Dynasty, or perhaps at the beginning of that of his son, Merenptah.

In my view, this conventional account contains serious errors and omissions. I believe that Joseph was by inheritance a prince of Egypt as well as the last Hebrew patriarch and was sold into slavery more than two centuries later than is generally accepted. The Pharaoh who appointed him as his vizier was Tuthmosis IV (*c.*1413–1405 BC), the eighth ruler of the Eighteenth Dynasty, who was very young—in his mid-twenties—when he died. He was succeeded by his son, Amenhotep III.

The line of descent in Egypt was through the eldest daughter and the eldest son married her to keep the title of Pharaoh in the family. Amenhotep III obtained the title to the throne by marrying his infant sister, Sitamun.[1] Before the second year of his reign, however, he broke with Egyptian tradition. There are indications that, in addition to the two sons we know of from the Bible, Joseph had a daughter. I believe that, against the advice of his priests, Amenhotep III married this daughter and made her, rather than Sitamun, his Great Royal Wife (queen). The precise relationship of the four Pharaohs who followed —Amenhotep IV (Akhnaten), Semenkhkare, Tutankhamun and Aye —has also been the subject of debate. Akhnaten is known to have been the son of Amenhotep III. Semenkhkare's skeleton suggests that he was about nineteen or twenty when he died, having served for three years as co-regent with Akhnaten, who was thirty-four at the time, and opinions differ as to whether he was Akhnaten's brother or son. Doubts also exist about whether Tutankhamun, who died nine years after Akhnaten at the age of about nineteen, was yet a third brother or the son of Akhnaten. It seems to me more likely that Akhnaten and Semenkhkare were brothers, in which case Joseph was their maternal grandfather, and Tutankhamun was the son of Akhnaten, in which case Joseph was his great-grandfather. No matter what the exact relationship, however, all three were descendants of Joseph. Finally, Tutankhamun was succeeded in his turn by Aye who, although complete proof is lacking, I believe to have been Joseph's second son.

I do not accept that the Israelites' sojourn in Egypt lasted four hundred and thirty years: it could not have been for more than a century, and I place the time of the Oppression and Exodus much earlier than is generally accepted—the Oppression during the reign of

---

[1] Scholars are virtually unanimous that Sitamun was Amenhotep III's daughter, not his sister. Although it is known that Amenhotep III had three sisters, one of whom was named Sitamun, she is said to have died in infancy, but the present writer does not accept this view (see Chapter 6). Furthermore, it was against Egyptian custom for Pharaohs to marry their own daughter.

Horemheb (*c*.1335–1308 BC), the last ruler of the Eighteenth Dynasty and the Exodus during the short reign of Ramses I (*c*.1308–1307 BC), first ruler of the Nineteenth. Finally, I do not believe that, at the time of the Exodus, Moses brought the bones of Joseph out of Egypt to bury them again in Palestine. In my opinion the remains of the Hebrew patriarch have never left Egypt and they are to be found today on the first floor of Cairo Museum in the shape of a mummy, largely forgotten and ignored, named Yuya.

I hasten to say that, in putting forward this interpretation of events, it is not my intention to undermine anybody's religious belief. Nor is it meant to be an attack upon the basic truths of either the Bible or the Koran. If anything, the opposite is the case: I hope to show that, when placed in a logical setting, certain Old Testament and koranic stories, which might be—and frequently are—dismissed as myths or allegories, prove to be, in fact, accounts of actual historical events. But first a brief explanation of how this book came to be written . . .

Its own genesis may be said to date from 1947, the year that marked the outbreak of the first hostilities between Egypt and the new state of Israel. I was thirteen at the time, a devout Muslim who said his prayers and read the Koran every morning. I would have been quite happy to fight and, if necessary, die for my God: it was a Holy War, and death in a Holy War meant an instant place in Paradise. I even went to a camp to volunteer, but I was turned away because I was too young.

By the time another round of hostilities threatened, in the early 1960s, my views had changed markedly. In the intervening years I had done my military service, studied law and found myself a job as a journalist. I had written four plays, one of which had been produced (the other three had been banned by the censor, who did not approve of public discussion of politics, religion or sex, restrictions that did not leave a great deal of scope for creative writing). I had also become absorbed in the apparently irrational enmity that existed between Egypt and Israel. Why could they not agree to live peacefully together? Why would they not settle their differences by talking instead of fighting? After all, the Jews were merely returning to their ancestors' homeland and could not be regarded as alien invaders like the French and British. It was their Holy Land as well as our Holy Land. The hostility between the two peoples struck me as being like a bitter, long-running family feud whose roots must lie buried in the deep past of our forgotten common history.

Trying to trace those roots was to occupy a great deal of my life for more than the next two decades. In the meantime, having done my military service and being liable for call-up, I felt I did not want to have any part of a struggle that would, quite reasonably, be looked upon by both sides as a Holy War. I flew to London and, except for visits, I have not been back to my own country since.

In London, where I made a living by teaching Arabic, I joined the Egypt Exploration Society and enrolled in a three-year evening course on the history of my native land. I spent another three years studying hieroglyphics. I also learned Hebrew, although that was not too difficult as, like Arabic, it is a Semitic language. All of this knowledge enabled me to delve deeply into ancient sources: yet it was to be a long-familiar text that inspired this book. One winter's night about four years ago I awoke in the early hours and found I could not sleep, so I made myself some tea and sat by the fire, reading again—as I often did, and still often do—the story of Joseph in the Old Testament. On this occasion I was struck suddenly by a passage in the Book of Genesis that I had passed over many times before without attaching any particular significance to it.

It occurs when, at a time of famine, Joseph's half-brothers make the second of two visits to Egypt to buy corn. On the first occasion, Joseph had concealed his true identity from the kinsmen who sold him into slavery: this time he reveals himself to them, but says reassuringly: 'So then it was not you who sent me hither, but God: and he hath made me a father to Pharaoh . . .' A father to Pharaoh! I found it difficult to believe that I had read those words so often in the past without attaching any real importance to them.

They could only be a title. Yet in what sense could Joseph be considered a father to Pharaoh? Pharaoh himself was looked upon, irrespective of his own age, as a father to all his people. Nor did it seem possible that Joseph was claiming a metaphorical title derived from his exalted position as vizier: for example, when Tutankhamun was not yet nineteen he had a vizier in his eighties who, despite the vast difference in their ages, is referred to as 'the son of the king in Kush.' My instinctive reaction was that the words meant precisely what they said, and my thoughts turned at once to Yuya. From the time of the Hyksos rulers, right through the New Kingdom that followed, Yuya is the only person we know of in the history of Egypt to bear the title 'a father to Pharaoh'. Although Yuya was not ostensibly of Royal blood,

his mummy was found in the early years of this century in the Valley of
the Kings, in a tomb between those of two Pharaohs. Could the
patriarch Joseph and this apparent stranger in the Valley of the Kings
be one and the same person?

I found the thought—perhaps intuition would be a more apt
word—almost frightening. For two or three centuries, scholars had
struggled to try to establish a historical connection between Old
Testament personalities and Egyptian history, to pin down someone as
having lived at a certain time, the cornerstone of a framework into
which other biblical personalities and events could be fitted. It was a
task that had not been made any easier by Egypt's loss of an enormous
part of the memories of its past in a single catastrophe when the
Alexandrian library, supposed to have contained some half a million
manuscripts, was destroyed by fire during a Roman assault on the city
in the first century BC, plus later depredations by Islamic conquerors,
armed with the Koran, who regarded all ancient writings as blasphem-
ous. The result of these centuries of scholarly effort had been some
small clues to a handful of places associated with the Sojourn and
Oppression, a possible time for the Exodus, one passing reference to
Israel. But where was Joseph? Where was Moses, said to have lived in
the Royal palace? Why had none of those eminent minds made the
connection between Joseph (Yussuf in the Koran) and Yuya, whose
names were so similar? I myself had been studying the Bible and the
history of Ancient Egypt for twenty years without doing so. Why
should I be given this insight when it had escaped so many distinguished scholars? Was I perhaps mistaken about the title that
appeared on one of the *ushabti*[1] in Yuya's tomb and more than a score
of times in his *Book of the Dead*?

I was so excited that I could not sleep. Dawn came and went, and I
was waiting outside the doors of the Egypt Exploration Society library
when it opened that same morning. Firstly, I checked the text of a
Hebrew edition of the Old Testament: it was quite specific, *wa-yašim-
ni la-ab la-Phar'a*, which translated literally means: 'And placed (set)
he me for a father to Pharaoh.' Then I turned to two books—
The Tomb of Iouiya and Touiyou by Theodore M. Davis, the rich
American who financed the exploration that led to the discovery of

---

[1] These small figures, resembling the mummy of the deceased, but with the head and
neck exposed, were placed in the tomb to act as substitutes for the dead person during
his time in the underworld.

Yuya's tomb, and *Funerary Papyrus of Iouiya* by Henri Naville, the distinguished Swiss Egyptologist. Davis records that the title *it nṯr n nb tawi*—the holy father of the Lord of the Two Lands (Lord of the Two Lands was Pharaoh's formal title)—occurs once on one of Yuya's *ushabti* (Royal funeral statuette No. 51028 in the Cairo Museum catalogue) and, as Naville confirms, more than twenty times on his funerary papyrus.

   Proving that Joseph and Yuya were the same person would clearly by a formidable task that meant challenging conventional scholarship, the accepted notion that the tribe of Israel spent four hundred and thirty years in Egypt, and the Bible's insistence that Moses brought the bones of Joseph with him for re-burial when he led the Exodus out of Egypt. Yet I felt that my intuition in the small hours of a cold winter's night would prove to be true—and might perhaps explain the almost mystical quality of the enmity that scars relations between Egypt and Israel.

Ahmed Osman,
London, 1987.

Book One

A FATHER TO PHARAOH

Chapter 1

THE TOMB OF YUYA

The tomb of Yuya and his wife, Tuya, was found in 1905, three years after Theodore M. Davis had obtained a concession to excavate in Biban el-Moluk, the Valley of the Kings, at Western Thebes. Davis, who took to spending the winters of his old age at Luxor in Upper Egypt, provided the money: the actual work was carried out by archaeologists, officials of the Service of Antiquities such as Howard Carter, James Quibell, Arthur Weigall and Edward Ayrton, all of whom were British and had been trained by Flinders Petrie, the first Englishman to dig in Egypt, whose work there over the next forty-two years was to make him a giant of modern archaeology.

In the Valley of the Kings there is a narrow side valley, about half a mile long, leading up to the mountain. At its mouth the tombs of a prince of Ramses III (c.1151–1132 BC) and Ramses XI (c. 1114–1087 BC) had been found earlier, dug into the side of a foothill about sixty feet high. In 1902, Howard Carter, who was then Inspector-General of the Antiquities of Upper Egypt and in charge of the new excavations, began to explore this valley, starting from the tomb of Ramses XI and working towards the mountain. The exploration proved rewarding in the following year, 1903, when Carter discovered the tomb of Tuthmosis IV, the father of Amenhotep III (c.1405–1367 BC). During the same twelve months it led to the unearthing of the tomb of another figure from the Eighteenth Dynasty, Queen Hatshepsut, who reigned from about 1490 to 1468 BC. After that, however, the trail went cold.

Eight days before the Christmas of 1904, Quibell replaced Carter to continue the examination of the side valley. The flanks of the hills were scraped over by the workmen until the loose upper surface of chips, natural and artificial, had been removed and the rock was bared. A month later, Davis arrived on the scene to learn that all this work had yielded nothing. He therefore decided, following Quibell's advice, to abandon the site and transfer the men back to the mouth of the side

valley, even if this, too, appeared to be an area that was unlikely to
yield any further discoveries. Davis records in his book *The Tomb of
Iouiya and Touiyou*, published in 1907: 'The site was most unpromising, lying as it did between the Ramses tombs (a prince of Ramses III
and Ramses XI) which had required so many men for so many years;
therefore it did not seem possible that a tomb could have existed in so
narrow a space without being discovered. As an original proposition I
would not have explored it, and certainly no Egyptologist, exploring
with another person's money, would have thought of risking the time
and expense. But I knew every yard of the lateral valley, except the
space described, and I decided that good exploration justified its
investigation, and that it would be a satisfaction to know the entire
valley, even if it yielded nothing.'

Back at the mouth of the valley, the workmen started cutting away
at the huge bank of chippings, about thirty feet high, that lay on the
side of the hill between the two Ramses tombs. After ten days they
struck the first indication of a third tomb in the shape of a well-cut
stone step that promised to prove the first of a flight descending to a
tomb passage. By February 11 they had exposed the top of a sealed
door protruding from the filling of limestone and sand that blocked the
stairwell. At this time Quibell had to leave the site and Arthur Weigall
took his place. Within twenty-four hours, the door, which was cut in
solid rock, had been entirely cleared. However, a section measuring
twelve inches by four inches near the top of the doorway had been
filled in with Nile mud plaster, an indication that the tomb had been
broken into at an earlier date by a robber.

Weigall's team decided to follow his example. They broke through
the seal at the top of the doorway in order to obtain a glimpse of what
lay inside. All they could see in the darkness was a steeply sloping
corridor about five feet wide. What lay beyond it? The aperture left by
the broken seal was too narrow to accommodate an adult, so they
enlisted the services of a small Egyptian boy and lowered him down
through the tiny opening. The boy brought out some small objects that
he had found lying on the floor a few feet from the doorway—a
gold-covered yoke from a chariot, a wooden staff of office and a scarab
(sacred beetle) that, at first glance, appeared to be of solid gold but, on
closer examination, proved to be a stone covered with a type of gold
foil.

Weigall and Davis were joined at the entrance to the tomb the next morning by Gaston Maspero, the Director-General of Cairo Museum. After workers had taken down the door, the three men, each carrying a candle, entered. They made their way down the steep corridor to find a second door. At the top it had an opening similar to that at the first, and it was covered from top to bottom with the stamps of the necropolis seal. By the foot of the door lay two pottery bowls in which the ancient workmen had mixed the final coat of plaster to close the tomb securely. Maspero and Davis used their bare hands to remove some of the stones from the top of the wall and peered through the hole. In the darkness they could see shining gold covering some kind of furniture that they were unable to identify. Impatient, they managed to scramble through the top of the second door without waiting for workmen to take it down, then descended into the darkness of the sepulchral chamber. The first thing, naturally, that they wanted to know was the name of the owner of the tomb.

'We held our candles, but they gave so little light and so dazzled our eyes that we could see nothing but the glitter of gold,' Davis recalled a few pages further on in his book. 'In a moment or two, however, I made out a very large funeral sled, which was used to contain all the coffins of the dead person and his mummy, and to convey them to his tomb. It was about six feet high and eight long, made of wood covered with bitumen, which was as bright as the day it was put on. Around the upper part of the coffin was a strip of gold foil, about six inches wide, covered with hieroglyphs. On (my) calling Monsieur Maspero's attention to it, he immediately handed me his candle, which, together with my own, I held before my eyes, close to the inscriptions so that he could read them. In an instant, he said: "Iouiya." Naturally excited by the announcement, and blinded by the glare of the candles, I involuntarily advanced them near the coffin; whereupon Monsieur Maspero cried out: "Be careful," and pulled my hands back. In a moment we realised that, had my candles touched the bitumen, which I came dangerously near to doing, the coffin would have been in a blaze.'

Davis's generous decision to continue exploring the unpromising site between the two Ramses tombs at the mouth of the valley produced a rich treasure trove of Egyptian antiquities. When electric light was introduced into the tomb it could be seen that it contained also the sarcophagus of Yuya's wife, Tuya. The relics recovered included:

Yuya's wooden sarcophagus, covered with black pitch and bearing lines of inscription, on a sledge.

Yuya's mummy inside three coffins (like that of Tutankhamun).

Tuya's wooden sarcophagus, on a sledge, with text mentioning her son, Anen, second prophet of the god Amun-Re.[1]

Two coffins, including Tuya's mummy.

Two gilt masks, one for each of the tomb occupants (this was the mask placed immediately over the head of the mummy).

Two canopic boxes, each divided into four compartments, in which the four canopic vases containing the viscera of the dead were placed.

Many *ushabti* in wooden boxes.

Yuya's staff and whip handle.

The handle of Tuya's sistrum, a jingling instrument or rattle used especially in the rites of Isis, wife of Osiris, the god of the dead, and also in the worship of Aten, god of the new religion, at Amarna (see Chapter 13).

Alabaster vases.

Dummy wooden vases.

A wooden statue with text from *The Book of the Dead*, a justification of the dead person's life which, among other things, included spells to help him on his journey through the underworld.

Three beautiful wooden chairs of different sizes, belonging to Sitamun.

A jewel box of Amenhotep III.

Two beds.

A chest belonging to Amenhotep III and his queen, Tiye.

An alabaster vase belonging to the king and queen.

A kohl tube—kohl was a form of make-up—with the name of Amenhotep III inscribed on it.

Pottery.

Clay sealing, thought to have the name of Ramses III,[2] attached to linen.

Yuya's necklace of large golden beads and lapis lazuli.

[1]Amun-Re was the supreme god of the Eighteenth Dynasty, the god of Thebes, accepted all over the country. He had four prophets, which was a priestly title. The first prophet was therefore the High Priest.

[2] *Topographical Bibliography of Ancient Egyptian Hieroglyphic Texts, Reliefs and Paintings*, Bertha Porter and Rosalind Moss.

    Toilet articles of various types.

    A plentiful supply of mummified meats, again meant to support the dead person on his or her journey through the underworld.

    A papyrus wig basket and a wig, probably of human hair.

    Pairs of sandals in two different sizes, varying in length from 18 to 30cm.

    A papyrus, 22 yards long, containing chapters of *The Book of the Dead*.

    A chariot, in perfect condition, which was at that time only the second chariot known to have survived from ancient Egypt.

Until the discovery of the tomb of Tutankhamun seventeen years later, the tomb of Yuya was the only one to be found almost intact in Egypt. The two mummies were lying in their coffins. Originally, Yuya's mummy had been enclosed in three coffins and Tuya's in two, but whoever had broken into the tomb earlier had evidently taken out the inner coffins and removed their lids. Looking for gold ornaments and jewels, he had scratched the mummy-cloth—stiff and hard from the unguents that had originally been poured over it and had then dried—with his nails, leaving a great quantity of small bits of cloth in both coffins.

When Yuya's body was lifted, the necklace of large beads, made of gold and lapis lazuli and strung on a strong thread, which had apparently been broken during the scratching of the mummy cloth, was found behind the mummy's neck. The tomb robber had also overlooked a gold plate, about the size of the palm of a man's hand, that had been inserted by the embalmer to conceal the incision he made in extracting Yuya's heart for special mummification. Both mummies were so well preserved that it seemed to Arthur Weigall as if they might open their eyes and speak.

The official opening of the tomb took place on February 13, 1905, attended by the King of England's brother, the Duke of Connaught, and his Duchess, who happened to be visiting Egypt at the time. Removing, cataloguing and packing the objects from the tomb, which was supervised by Quibell, took three weeks. Despite all the care taken, some of the packers managed to steal objects from the tomb, but all are believed to have been recovered through buying them back from dealers.[1] On March 3, one hundred and twenty workmen started to carry the packing cases down to the river, where they were left

[1]*Catalogue général des antiquités égyptiennes du Musée du Caire*, James E. Quibell.

overnight before being loaded onto a guarded train, bound for Cairo and Yuya's present resting place in the Egyptian capital's museum.

Although the tomb of Yuya and Tuya was the most complete one to be found before that of Tutankhamun, nobody thought that Yuya personally was of any great importance. Davis wrote his account of the discovery, with an introduction by Maspero, in 1907: Naville published his study of Yuya's *Book of the Dead* a year later. Nothing much has been done since, other than some studies of different pieces of the funerary furniture and its texts. Yet in the case of Yuya there are enough curious facets to make it surprising that his origins were not the subject of more detailed investigation, either at the time or in the intervening eighty years.

As we have already seen, he is the only person we know of from the time of the Hyksos kings onward to bear the title *it ntr n nb tawi*—the holy father of the Lord of the Two Lands (Pharaoh), the same title claimed by Joseph—and, although not apparently of Royal blood, he was buried in the Valley of the Kings rather than in the Valley of the Nobles, close to the village of Sheikh Abdel Korna. Furthermore, unlike the tombs of other nobles, Yuya's was neither decorated nor inscribed; his name, found on his sarcophagus, the three coffins and other pieces of funerary furniture, is not Egyptian and had not been discovered in Egypt before that time; unlike the ears of most Royal mummies of the New Kingdom, Yuya's were not pierced, and the position of his hands, the palms facing his neck under the chin, is different from the usual Osiris form in which the dead man's hands are crossed over his chest. Yuya, as far as is known, is the only Egyptian mummy to have been found with his hands in this position.

Yuya bore an impressive list of titles in addition to 'the holy father of the Lord of the Two Lands':

> Father of the God, or Holy Father (This was a common priestly title which might be said to correspond to the 'Father' of the Roman Catholic Church and the High Church of England or the 'Padre' of the armed forces),
> Master of the Horse,
> Deputy of His Majesty in the Chariotry,
> Bearer of the ring of the King of Lower Egypt,
> Seal-bearer of the King of Lower Egypt,
> Hereditary Noble and Count,

Overseer of the Cattle of Min, Lord of Akhmim,
Overseer of the Cattle of Amun,
Favourite of the Good God (Pharaoh),
Confidant of the King,
Confidant of the Good God,
Mouth of the King of Upper Egypt,
Ears of the King of Lower Egypt,
Prophet of the God Min,
Sole Friend (Unique Friend),
First of the Friends,
Prince,
Great Prince,
Great of Love,
Plentiful of Favours in the House of the King,
Plentiful of Favours under his Lord,
Enduring of Love under his Lord,
Beloved of the King of Upper Egypt,
Beloved of the King of Lower Egypt,
Beloved of the Lord of the Two Lands,
Beloved of God,
Possessor of Favour under the Lord of the Two Lands,
Praised of the Good God,
Praised of his God,
Praised of his Lord,
Praised of his Lord Amun,
Praised of the King,
Praised of the Lord of the Two Lands,
Praised One who came forth from the Body Praised,
One made rich by the King of Lower Egypt,
One made great by the King of Lower Egypt,
One made great by the Lord who does things,
First among the King's Companions,
The Wise One,
He whom the King made Great and Wise, whom the King has
    made his Double.

Unlike his wife, Tuya, who had conventional Egyptian looks, Yuya was remarkably foreign in appearance, as Arthur Weigall recorded in his book *The Life and Times of Akhnaten*, published in 1910: 'He was a person of commanding presence, whose powerful character showed itself in his face. One must picture him now as a tall man, with a fine shock of white hair; a great hooked nose like that of a Syrian; full, strong lips; and a prominent, determined jaw. He has the face of an ecclesiastic, and there is something about his mouth which reminds one of the late Pope, Leo XIII. One feels on looking at his well-preserved features, that there may be found the originator of the great religious movement which his daughter and grandson carried into execution.'

This was a reference to Tiye, the daughter of Yuya and Tuya, whom Amenhotep III made his Great Royal Wife, and their son, Amenhotep IV (Akhnaten), who was to close the temples, destroy the gods of Egypt and establish in their place a monotheistic God, like the God of Israel (see Chapter 8).

Chapter 2

VOICES FROM THE PAST

The two basic sources for the story of Joseph are the Old Testament and the Koran, and it is a tradition common to Jews, Muslims and Christians alike that the contents of both books have as their source the inspired word of God, handed down to prophets. The question of how the Old Testament has reached us has been the subject of continuing debate for two thousand years, with the areas of discussion including the number of original sources it had, when it was first written down and by whom, the degree to which it has been tampered with over the centuries and to what extent it is to be regarded as describing actual historical events.

Without going into the matter in detail at this stage (see Book Two, Chapter One), a turning point in the history of biblical criticism came when Jean Astruc (1684–1766), the physician to Louis XV, published a treatise on the Book of Genesis in 1753, suggesting that Moses compiled the Pentateuch—the first five books of the Old Testament —from two documentary sources that had been transmitted over several centuries, either orally or in written form, and reassembled the ancient memories so as to furnish a continuous narrative. Astruc also pointed out that Genesis contained two versions of the Creation story while the account of the Deluge showed evidence of two different narratives having been compounded into one. What was to inspire a new approach to the whole subject of the Old Testament, however, was his observation that, both in Genesis and the early chapters of Exodus, God was referred to by two different names, Elohim and Jehovah *(Yhwh)*.

Astruc's ideas, developed by Old Testament scholars, chiefly from Germany, in the first half of the nineteenth century, led to the definitive attribution of the contents of the Pentateuch to four different sources. These scholars were followed by K. H. Graf, who suggested in 1865 that the sections using the name Elohim, then assumed to be the

earliest of the sources, was, in fact, the later document, compiled at the
time of Ezra when Jewish scholars returned after the enforced exile of
more than a century that had followed the Babylonian conquest of
Canaan. It was because of this attempt by Graf to assign dates to the
different documents that a new branch of study emerged, historical
criticism. The final development of the German school's work was left
to a man of wide spiritual vision, Julius Wellhausen (1844–1918),
whose brilliant and penetrating mind led him to a prominent position
in the field of Old Testament criticism, similar to that of Darwin
in the biological sciences. Like Darwin, Wellhausen adopted the
Hegelian idea of evolution and developed Graf's theories to what he
thought was their natural conclusion. He regarded the Pentateuch as
essentially of composite origin, consisting of:

1   A Jehovistic source (J), dating from the ninth century BC.
2   An Elohistic document (E), dating from the eighth century BC.
3   The book of Deuteronomy (D), to be regarded as a separate
    source, dating from the seventh century BC.
4   A priestly source (P), dating from about the fifth century BC.
5   The work of an editor who revised and edited the entire
    collection around the second century BC.

More recently, Professor Donald B. Redford of Toronto University,
in his book *A Study of the Biblical Story of Joseph*, has concluded that
all the historical indications relating to Joseph and the Descent,
including every reference to Egypt and Egyptian names, locations and
titles, are pure inventions of the biblical editor, who wanted to justify
the Exodus by bringing Joseph and the Israelites into Egypt. His
conclusions mean that Joseph as we know him never existed. Some
modern scholars have also challenged Wellhausen's method of source
analysis—without suggesting an alternative—in its application to
books that follow the Pentateuch. In the Pentateuch itself, however, it
is Wellhausen's ideas that still capture the main body of contemporary
biblical critics and his arguments still form the basis of biblical studies
today.

One indication in the Bible itself of two parallel documentary
sources behind the story of Joseph is that his father, Jacob, is referred
to fifteen times by this name and fifteen times as Israel, the new name
given to him by the Lord. Similarly, the name of the dominant 'good
brother', who protected Joseph from death and had him sold into

slavery in Egypt instead, not only varies between Reuben and Judah, but Reuben occurs each time that the name Jacob is used and Judah each time that the name Israel is used. Further evidence that the Old Testament, even in its final, complete version, existed in more than one form, was provided by discovery of the Dead Sea Scrolls—fragments, and sometimes complete scrolls, from the books of the Old Testament, dating back to the second century BC—in Qumran in 1947. Scholars were surprised to discover that, although most of the Dead Sea Scrolls agreed with the Hebrew text tradition, some of the material they contained reinforced the Greek text—the Septuagint, which is older than the Hebrew Massoretic text—as well, while others differed from both, indicating that at the time, the second and first centuries BC, there were more than two versions of the Old Testament text in circulation among the Jews of Palestine.

This brief outline of the development of biblical criticism makes it clear, I think, that the Old Testament—and, in particular, the five books of the Pentateuch, which is our main concern—ought to be approached with a mixture of caution and common sense. Although I am neither a Jew nor a Christian myself, as a Muslim I accept that the Old Testament is the inspired word of God, and that any story it contains would not be there unless it were both important and significant. At the same time one must make allowances for the fact that these stories were originally handed down over several centuries by word of mouth, with the inevitable distortions, and possible accretions, that this would involve; that priests and editors have made their contribution to the text we know today; that translators have inserted interpolations, based on their own concept of morality; the inherent difficulties of translation itself (one Hebrew word may need a dozen English words to render its precise meaning), and the fact that the language used in biblical times was vastly different from the language we use today.

The story of Joseph and his family that follows is a condensed version of the account that appears in the Pentateuch. In the process of condensing it I have concentrated on the essentials that are necessary for historical inquiry. This is not a question of simply choosing texts that suit my argument, but of trying to get to the heart of the matter. To give two convenient examples, it is part of the narrative that a man fell in love with the younger daughter but had first to marry the elder one, that being the custom, but I do not feel there is any point in wasting time on the unlikely proposition—which Genesis provides for us—that he did not realise until the morning after the wedding that he was married to the wrong bride. Similarly, in the case of the twin who sold his birthright for a mess of pottage, the essence of the story is the sale of the birthright, and what it might have been, rather than whether a bowl of soup formed the basis of the transaction, except insofar as a bowl of soup suggests that the seller did not value his birthright very highly.

I have also devoted little time, space or importance to biblical dates and ages, subjects on which the Old Testament is notoriously wayward. It would have us believe that the world was created at a time when we know from other evidence that the earth was already inhabited. We read of people living for more than a century in an era when forty or fifty was considered a good lifespan. It may be, of course, that they attached a different meaning than we do to the word 'year', but even this does not serve to explain errors in biblical chronology in such cases as that of Terah, Joseph's great-great-grandfather, who is said to have been seventy when his son, Abram, was born. Terah, we are then told, proceeded to live to the ripe age of two hundred and five. Yet a few verses further on we learn that Abram was still only seventy-five when his father died. And so to the story of Joseph. To understand it fully, however, we have to go back three generations to the time of his great-grandfather, Abram, the founder of the Hebrew tribes into which Moses, Jesus and Muhammad would be born many centuries later . . .

The entrance to the tomb of Yuya in the Valley of the Kings, discovered by James Quibell and Theodore Davis in 1905, situated between the tombs of Ramses III and Ramses XI.

Yuya's sarcophagus, lacking the elaborate decoration of others of the same period. *Photo: Cairo Museum*

The sarcophagus of Yuya's wife, Tuya. *Photo: Cairo Museum*

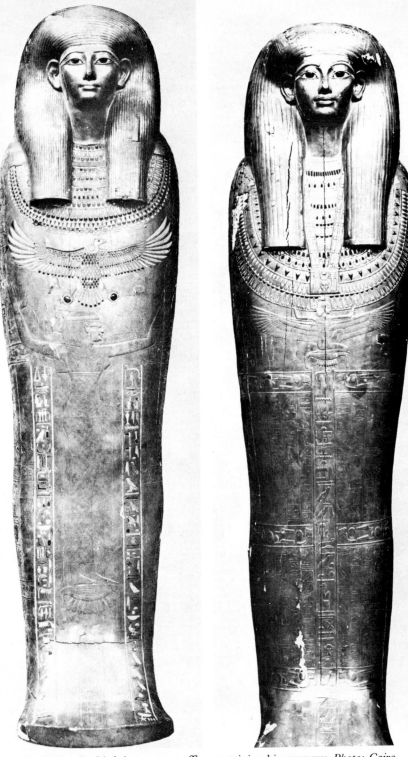

(Left) Yuya's third, innermost coffin, containing his mummy. *Photo: Cairo Museum*

(Right) Tuya's inner coffin. Unlike her husband, she had only two. *Photo: Cairo Museum*

Details of the upper parts of Tuya's outer (left) and inner coffins. *Photos: Cairo Museum*

Tuya's golden mask. This was placed directly over the mummy's head. *Photo: Cairo Museum*

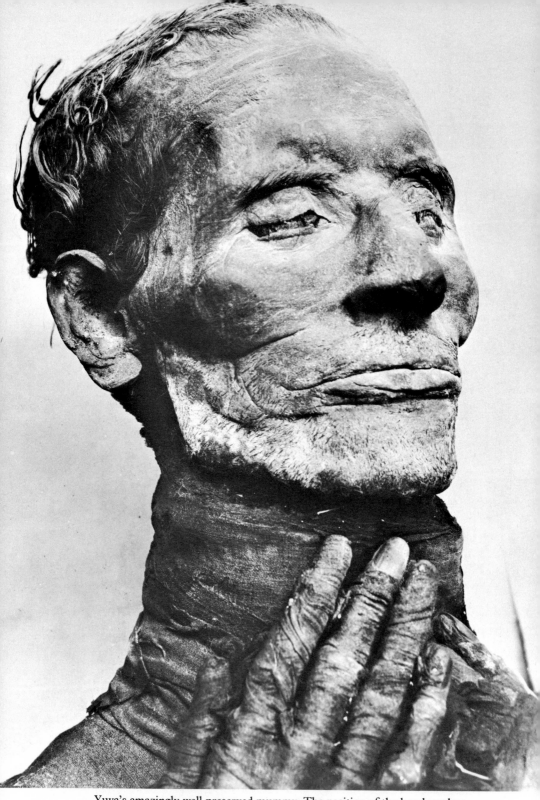

Yuya's amazingly well preserved mummy. The position of the hands, palms down under the chin, is unique in Ancient Egypt; the ears, unusually, are unpierced. *Photo: Cairo Museum*

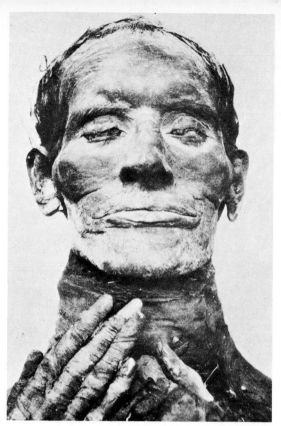

Frontal and profile views of Yuya's mummy. His strong, aquiline features and hooked nose suggested at once to those who examined the mummy that he was of foreign, possibly Semitic, origin. His white hair and aged appearance indicated that he was at least sixty years old when he died. *Photos: Cairo Museum*

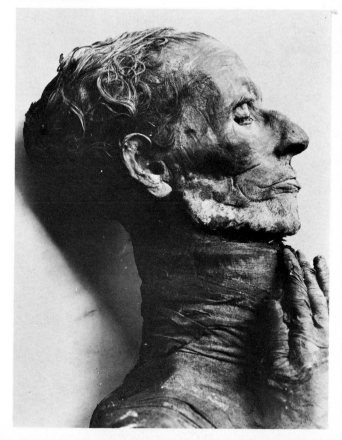

Two views of Tuya's mummy. Unlike her husband, her features are more typically Egyptian, and her ears are pierced. *Photos: Cairo Museum*

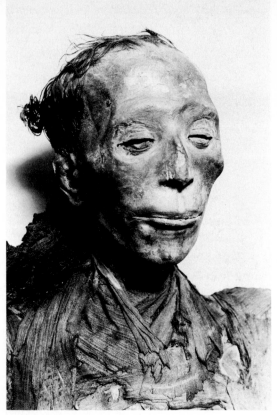

Chapter 3

A SPECIAL FAMILY

The first mention of Joseph's family in the Bible occurs in the Book of Genesis, immediately after the account of the Creation, the Fall and the Deluge. Genesis records the migration of Abram, his wife, Sarai, his father, Terah, and his nephew, Lot, from Ur in Mesopotamia, not far from what was then the head of the Persian Gulf, to Canaan. Canaan at that time occupied much the same area as modern Israel and Lebanon, and was some 750 miles from Ur by the great trade route that followed the valley of the Euphrates north-west through Babylon to Mari, then swept west through Syria to the eastern shores of the Mediterranean.

Abram and Sarai made the journey in two stages. They settled for a while at Haran, in the middle of the valley of the Euphrates, but, after Terah's death, the Lord said to Abram: 'Leave your country, your people and your father's household and go to the land I shall show you.' So they continued their journey to Canaan, a country where the sudden appearance of strangers was a common occurrence. It stood at the crossroads of what we now call the Near East. Traders used its coastal plain for their commercial journeys south to, and north from, Egypt. It also afforded passage to armies during the recurrent imperialist rivalries between Egypt on the one hand and Assyria and Babylon on the other. In addition, at times of semi-drought the country suffered mini-invasions by tribesmen from the neighbouring desert.

For anyone trying to make a living from the soil, Canaan posed an intimidating challenge. The climate was hostile. In summer the country was scorched by the sun and the hot, sand-laden sirocco wind from the desert. The late autumn rains, which made it possible to plough the baked soil, were followed by wet, and often bitterly cold, winters. Then, as the sun grew in strength, the gentler rains of March and April provided a little fresh pasture for sheep, goats and cattle before the onset of another dry season.

Grain could be grown only on the coastal plain and in the valleys, and the staple agricultural products of the country, all that the inhospitable stony hills would support, were the olive and the vine. Famine was a regular occurrence, and it was at a time of famine that Abram and Sarai set out on their travels again, making their way down to Egypt, a journey that was to forge the first links between the Egyptian Royal house and, as it was later to become, the tribe of Israel, the Chosen People according to both the Bible and the Koran.

Compared to Canaan, Egypt was a rich and sophisticated country. While the greater part of it was desert, the land on either side of the Nile, watered by an intricate system of irrigation canals and dykes, and the land of the river's delta, flooded each year by the inundation that followed heavy rains and melting snows in the Ethiopian Highlands, were exceptionally fertile. Major crops included wheat (for bread), barley (for beer), vegetables, fruit (including grapes for wine), flax (for linseed oil and linen thread). The soil was so rich that two crops could often be harvested in the same growing season. The Egyptians also kept pigs, goats, sheep, geese and ducks, and could supplement their diet with fish from the Nile, wild fowl from the marshes and game from the desert.

Although Abram and Sarai set out on the journey south of Egypt at a time of famine, it may have been some other motive—trade, perhaps —that caused them to make the trip. Certainly they did not stay in the eastern delta of the Nile, which one might have expected if they were simply seeking food, but made their way to wherever the Pharaoh of the time was holding court. This may have been in the palaces at Heliopolis or Memphis, both not far from present-day Cairo, or in the third palace at Thebes on the Upper Nile.

Sarai was a beautiful woman and Abram was understandably afraid that he might be murdered if Pharaoh coveted her. Before they entered Egypt he took the precaution of suggesting: 'Tell them that you are my sister, so that I shall be treated well for your sake and my life will be spared because of you.' In the event, it proved a wise provision. Once the courtiers of Pharaoh saw how beautiful Sarai was, she was taken to the Royal palace where she became Pharaoh's bride. Abram found himself rewarded generously for the hand of his 'sister'. He was given sheep and cattle, male and female donkeys, camels, menservants and maidservants, but marriage to another man's wife turned out less happily for Pharaoh. The Lord 'inflicted serious diseases' on him and his household, and, once he realised the cause of his problems, Pharaoh summoned Abram and asked: 'What have you done to me? Why didn't you tell me she is your wife? Why did you say, "She is my sister", so that I took her as my wife?[1] Now then, here is your wife. Take her and be gone.'

Abram and Sarai returned to Canaan, and from this point some fundamental changes begin to take place in a small tribe that, until then, had had no historical importance. The Lord appeared to Abram in a vision and prophesied: 'Know for certain that your descendants will be aliens living in a land that is not theirs, and they will be enslaved and ill-treated four hundred years ... The fourth generation will return here ...' God also made a covenant with Abram, saying: 'To your descendants I give this land, from the river of Egypt to the great river, the Euphrates ...'

Later, in another visitation, the Lord told Abram: '... No longer will you be called Abram; your name will be Abraham, for I have made you a father of a host of nations ... kings will come from you.'[2] He also said: 'Every male among you shall be circumcised. You shall circumcise the flesh of your foreskin, and it will be the sign of the covenant between me and you.' This command, which Abraham carried out, forged another link between the Hebrew tribe and Egypt, for, until that moment in history, only Egyptians among the eastern nations had adopted the custom of circumcision. At the same time, Sarai's name was changed as well. God said to Abraham: 'As for Sarai your wife ... her name will be Sarah. I shall bless her and give you a son by her ... kings of peoples will come from her.' *Sar* in Hebrew means prince and *sarah* is the feminine form, which can even be interpreted to mean 'the queen'. The Amarna

[1] The King James version of this exchange reads 'so I might have taken her to me to wife'. The interpolation of the words 'might have' implies that Pharaoh had not yet married Sarai when he discovered that she was Abram's wife. This seems to be one example of biblical translators applying their own morality values. The Hebrew original makes it clear that the marriage between Pharaoh and Sarai had already taken place. That is why Abram was given Sarai's dowry and why Pharaoh's house was plagued.

[2] If one looks at this from the point of view of Egyptian hieroglyphics, the insertion of the *ha* into Abram's name gives us *ham* (majesty) and his new name can be translated as 'heart of the majesty of the sun-god Re'.

letters[1] make it clear that Pharaoh himself was sometimes addressed as *sar*. It was the term, for instance, that Tarkhun Dara, the Hittite prince, used in addressing Amenhotep III.[2]

The promise that 'kings of peoples' would descend from Sarah is the first mention of any Hebrew kings. Until that time the Hebrews had lived in nomadic tribes, moving from place to place in search of food. The tribal society does not have a king, not even a prince, but only a chief, the head of the tribe.

Abraham was surprised to learn that Sarah would bear a son, partly because of their respective ages, partly because Sarah had been unable to conceive throughout their married life. In fact, to compensate for her own barrenness Sarah had given him her Egyptian maid Hagar, by whom he had a son, Ishmael, followed by another six sons by a second wife, Keturah. With the promise of a son for Sarah, Abraham felt the time was appropriate to make a plea on behalf of his first-born, Ishmael, and said: 'If only Ishmael could live under your blessing.'

God replied: 'Yes, but your wife Sarah will bear you a son, and you will call him Isaac. I shall establish my covenant with him as an everlasting covenant for his descendants after him. And as for Ishmael, I have heard you. I shall surely bless him; I shall make him fruitful and greatly increase his numbers. He will be the father of twelve princes, and I shall raise a great nation from him. But my covenant I shall establish with Isaac, whom Sarah will bear you by this time next year.' This passage makes it clear that Isaac was to be looked upon as Abraham's true heir. It was through him that the glory of the Hebrew tribe would be fulfilled and Israel would be born, of his seed that kings would rule from the Nile to the Euphrates.

The critical question, upon which everything else turns, is: *Who was Isaac's father?* As Sarah was married to both Abraham and Pharaoh,

[1] The Amarna letters are dozens of tablets of baked clay that a peasant woman stumbled upon in the ruins of the Egyptian city of Tell el Amarna in 1887. Hoping that they might prove valuable, she packed them into a sack, doing considerable damage in the process, and delivered them to a dealer in antiquities. It was only gradually, however, that scholars began to grasp the importance of the find. The tablets, written in the diplomatic language Akkadian, were basically the foreign archives of the Eighteenth Dynasty rulers of Egypt.

[2] *The Tell Amarna Tablets*, C. R. Conder. The princes of the five major Philistine cities, Gaza, Askalon, Ashdod, Gath and Ekron are referred to in the Hebrew Bible as *seren*, a Philistine word from the same root as *sar* (*The World of the Old Testament*, Cyrus H. Gordon). Caesar is another title from the same source.

the child could have belonged to either of them. However, if he was the son of Abraham, it is impossible to make any kind of logical and historical sense of the Old Testament story of Joseph and his family: it is only if Isaac was the son of Pharaoh, a prince of Egypt, that everything else falls into place.

It is interesting in this context that the Talmud, the Jewish commentaries and interpretive writings that are looked upon as only second in authority to the Old Testament, suggest that, when born, Isaac did not look like Abraham: 'On the day that Abraham weaned his son Isaac, he made a great banquet, and all the peoples of the world derided him, saying: "Have you see that old man and the woman who brought a foundling from the street, and now claim him as their son! And what is more they make a great banquet to establish their claim."' The account then strikes a miraculous note, doubts about whether Isaac was actually Abraham's son having the result that 'immediately the lineaments of Isaac's visage changed and became like Abraham's, whereupon they all cried out: "Abraham begat Isaac."'[1]

After the birth of Isaac, we have a curious episode where Abraham builds an altar, places the bound Isaac upon it and is about to slaughter him with a knife as a sacrifice to the Lord when a voice cries out from heaven: 'Do not raise your hand against the boy.' Apart from the fact that such human sacrifices were not the custom of the time, it is even more difficult to believe the story if Isaac was indeed Abraham's own son, and there is a much truer ring to the story in the Haggadah, the legendary part of the Talmud, that news of Abraham's intentions caused Sarah's death.

According to the Talmud, an old man approached Sarah near her tent and told her: 'Knowest thou that Abraham has offered up thy Isaac as a sacrifice before the Lord. Aye, despite his struggles and his cries, thy son has been made a victim to the knife.' The grief-stricken Sarah set out in search of Abraham and Isaac, but failed to find them. The account ends: 'Returning to her tents she was met by the same old man who had before addressed her, and thus he spoke: "Verily I did inform thee falsely, for Isaac, thy son, lives." Sarah's heart was stronger for grief than joy . . . she died and was gathered to her people.'[2] (See also Book Two, Chapter One.)

[1] *The Babylonian Talmud*, translated by Rabbi Dr I. Epstein.
[2] *Selections from the Talmud*, translated from the original by H. Polano.

The question of Isaac's parentage and the threatened sacrifice seems also to have a significant echo in a discussion that took place many centuries later between Jesus and the Jews. This is how the episode is described in the Gospel of St John (8:31–44):

'To the Jews who had believed him, Jesus said: "If you hold to my teaching, you are really my disciples. Then you will know the truth and the truth will set you free." They answered him: "We are Abraham's descendants and have never been slaves of anyone. How can you say that we shall be set free?" Jesus replied: "I tell you the truth, everyone who sins is a slave to sin. Now a slave has no permanent place in the family, but a son belongs to it for ever. So if the Son sets you free, you will be free indeed. I know you are Abraham's descendants. Yet you are ready to kill me, because you have no room for my word. I am telling you what I have seen in the Father's presence, and you do what you have heard from your father."

'"Abraham is our father," they answered.

'"If you were Abraham's children," said Jesus, "then you would do the things that Abraham did. As it is, you are determined to kill me, a man who has told you the truth that he heard from God. Abraham did not do such things. You are doing the things your own father does."

'"We are not illegitimate children," they protested. "The only Father we have is God Himself."

'Jesus said to them: "If God were your Father, you would love me, for I came from God and now am here. I have not come on my own, but He sent me. Why is not my language clear to you? Because you are unable to hear what I say. You belong to your father, the devil, and you want to carry out your father's desire. He was a murderer from the beginning, not holding to the truth, for there is no truth in him . . ."'

Here, instead of referring to Israel as their father, the Jews name Abraham because this was the disputed point. It is clear that the Jews have accepted in their argument that they were not physically the descendants of Abraham. Instead, they are the spiritual children of God. It seems that Jesus is wondering why, when Abraham did not kill Isaac, the Jews want to kill Him when he tells them he is the son of God. This confrontation between Jesus and the Jews appears to have been misinterpreted as anti-Semitic by some biblical scholars. In fact, what Jesus is telling them is that, if they refuse to behave like Abraham, they will be the followers of the murderous Devil.

When Isaac grew to manhood, he took a wife, Rebekah. Like Sarah before her, she was beautiful but barren.[1] However, Isaac prayed to the Lord on her behalf and she became pregnant with twins, both boys. The first to be born was named Esau, the second Jacob (*Y'qwb* means 'the one who follows'). The most intriguing aspect of their early life is Esau's sale of his birthright. The special blessing of the elder son is a theme that we find repeated in many biblical stories, but this is the only case where a birthright is mentioned. To what exactly did this right entitle its owner? The only logical explanation would be the inheritance of property or title. We know from the story in Genesis that Jacob did not receive any of Isaac's property after his father's death: the only apparent alternative, therefore, is that the birthright that passed from Esau, the elder twin, to Jacob, the younger, was the princely title belonging to their father.

Such a sale or transfer of a birthright is possible only in a society that does not consider primogeniture as the sole criterion for determining inheritance, and the Nuzi tablets demonstrate that other criteria were sometimes used in biblical times. Nuzi was the ancient city in northeast Iraq at the present site of Yoghlan Tepe, near the foothills of southern Kurdistan and about five miles south-west of Arrapkha (modern Kirkuk). Excavations began at Nuzi in 1925 and continued for six years under the joint auspices of the American School of Oriental Research, Harvard University, and the University Museum of Pennsylvania. More than four thousand tablets, written documents from public and private archives, were found and are now in the Oriental Institute of the University of Chicago and the Harvard Semitic Museum. One of these documents concerns a man who transferred his rights to his brother for three sheep.

In passing, it is worth noting that the Nuzi tablets also make it clear that Abram was probably not lying when he introduced Sarai as his sister on their arrival in Egypt. The wife-sister relationship was very rare outside of Egypt in ancient times, but the Nuzi documents show that in the Hurrian Society, of which both Nuzi and Haran were part, a

---

[1] Barren women who later have children are a recurrent feature in Abraham's story as well as elsewhere in the Old Testament. This may be simply an extravagant scriptural way of saying that, at a time when early marriage was the norm, a girl had been taken as a bride long before she reached child-bearing age. Tiye, for example, is thought to have been only about eight when Amenhotep III made her his Great Royal Wife, and the Prophet Muhammad married a nine-year-old girl when he himself was fifty.

Western Asia in the Amarna Age

wife-sister judicial status existed whereby a woman, in addition to becoming a man's wife, was adopted by him as a sister. In such cases, two separate documents were drawn up, one for marriage and the other for sistership, and the woman concerned merited higher social status and greater privileges than an ordinary wife.[1] But to return to the story of Abraham's descendants . . .

As I suggested earlier, the price Esau accepted for his birthright – 'a mess of pottage' – is best interpreted as an indication that he did not value his birthright very highly. It cannot have been easy for either him or Jacob, leading a simple nomadic life with their flocks, to believe the promises made to Abraham and Sarah that one day their descendants would rule over a vast kingdom. Yet, of the two, it seems likely from the Old Testament that Jacob would have had more faith in the fulfilment of the promises at some unknown time in the future. We know from the Book of Genesis that the two brothers had vastly different characters. Esau was 'a skilful hunter, a man of the open country': in contrast, Jacob, like the son Joseph who would be born to him, seems to have been more of a dreamer, 'a quiet man, staying among the tents'.

Once again, the Talmud offers confirmation: 'Then Isaac died, and Jacob and Esau wept together for their father's demise. They carried his body to the cave of Machpelah, which is in Hebron, and all the kings of Canaan followed with the mourners in the funeral train of Isaac . . . Isaac bequeathed his cattle and all his possessions to his two sons. Esau said then to Jacob: "Behold, this which our father has left us must be divided into two portions, then I will select my share." Jacob divided all his father's possessions into two portions in the presence of Esau and his sons, and then addressing his brother, said: ". . . Behold, the God of Heaven and Earth spoke unto our ancestors, Abraham and Isaac, saying, 'Unto thy seed will I give this land as an everlasting possession.' Now all that our father left is before thee; if thou desirest the promised possession, the land . . . take it and this other wealth shall be mine; or if thou desirest these two portions, be it as it is pleasing in thy eyes, and the land . . . shall be the share for me and mine."

'Before Esau replied and made his choice, he sought Nebaioth, the son of Ishmael, who was in that country, and asked his advice as to the selection. Nebaioth answered, "Behold, the Canaanites are now living

[1] *Encyclopaedia Judaica.*

in the land of peace and safety; at present it is theirs; let Jacob believe that he may inherit it some day; take thou the substance, the personal wealth of thy father." Esau followed this advice, and taking the personal substance he gave Jacob for his portion the land . . . from the river of Egypt unto the great river, the river Euphrates . . .'[1]

The loss of his birthright, followed by a subsequent disagreement over their father's blessing, rankled with Esau, who eventually threatened to kill Jacob. When their mother heard of the threat she sent for Jacob and told him: 'Your brother Esau is threatening to kill you. Now then, my son, do what I say. Flee at once to my brother Laban in Haran. Stay with him for a while until your brother's anger cools.'

Jacob took her advice and received a generous welcome from his uncle when he arrived at Haran. After he had been there for a month, Laban said to him: 'Just because you are a kinsman, why should you work for me for nothing? Tell me what your wages should be.' In the short time he had been at Haran, Jacob had already fallen in love with his cousin, Rachel, Laban's beautiful younger daughter, and he agreed to work for his uncle for seven years in return for her hand in marriage. At the end of the seven years, however, Laban gave Jacob his elder daughter, Leah, explaining: 'It is not our custom to give the younger daughter in marriage before the elder one. Finish out this daughter's seven-day bridal feast: then we shall give you the younger one as well, in return for another seven years' work.'

Jacob accepted the offer. After their marriage, Rachel, too, proved to be barren, but in the course of the years Jacob fathered eleven children—six sons and a daughter by Leah, two sons by Rachel's maid, Bilhah, and two more sons by Leah's maid, Zilpah. At last Rachel, his first love, gave him an eleventh son. They named him Joseph.

Soon afterwards, Jacob decided to return to his homeland, Canaan. On the way he had a mysterious encounter with a stranger, who wrestled with him all night and, when the struggle was finally broken off at daybreak, said: 'Your name will no longer be Jacob, but Israel, because you have struggled with God and with men and have prevailed.' There is a mystical element about this passage, but its significant aspect is the changing of Jacob's name to Israel. The Hebrew term

---

[1] *Selections from the Talmud*, translated by H. Polano.

el is the short form of Elohim (God) and *Ysra* or *sar* indicates a prince or a ruler. *Ysrael* means Elohim rules (Pharaoh, too, was looked upon as a ruling god). Jacob's new name therefore connected him both with Royalty and with his grandmother Sarah—and, as the change took place just after the birth of Joseph, Jacob must have taken it as a sign that the newly-born baby was his rightful heir.

Chapter 4

A SPECIAL SON

The account of the change in Jacob's name occurs in Chapter 32 of the Book of Genesis; the story of Joseph begins five chapters later, when he is seventeen years of age, and occupies virtually all the remainder of the Book.

Jacob, we are told, loved Joseph more than he loved any of his other sons and made a richly ornamented robe for him. His half-brothers hated Joseph because of this favouritism, and they hated him even more when he related a dream he had had. 'We were binding sheaves of corn in the field when suddenly my sheaf rose and stood upright, while your sheaves gathered round mine and bowed low to it,' he explained.

'Do you think one day you will lord it over us?' the angry brothers asked. Then Joseph had a second dream, which he related to his father as well as his brothers: 'I had another dream, and this time the sun, the moon and eleven stars were bowing down to me.' It served to fuel the brothers' jealousy, and Jacob rebuked Joseph, saying: 'What is this dream of yours? Must your mother and I and your brothers come and bow down to the ground before you?' Yet he did not forget what Joseph had said.

The early stories of the patriarchs were kept alive in the memory of Hebrew generations. Joseph's brothers must therefore have been aware of the birthright their father had bought from their uncle, Esau, and, even if they, too, did not really believe that a member of the family would rule one day over the land between the Nile and Euphrates, must have further resented their father's favourable treatment of Joseph on the grounds that it suggested the birthright was being passed on to him.

Joseph was at home with his father one day while the brothers were supposedly grazing their sheep near Shecham. Jacob said to him: 'Go and see if all is well with your brothers and with the sheep, and bring word back to me.' Joseph set off, but on arriving at Shecham could find no trace of his brothers and their sheep. A stranger told him: 'They have moved on from here. I heard them say: "Let's go down to Dothan."' Joseph went after them and, when they saw him approaching in the distance, they said to each other: 'Here comes that dreamer. Let's kill him and throw him into one of these pits and say that a wild animal devoured him. Then we'll see what comes of his dreams.'

Reuben, the eldest of the brothers, protested. 'Let's not take his life,' he said. 'Don't shed any blood.' When Joseph arrived on the scene, the brothers stripped him of his richly ornamented robe and threw him into an empty pit before sitting down to eat their meal. The ultimate outcome of the situation does not seem to have been decided until later, when they looked up and saw a caravan of Ishmaelites, their camels laden with spices, balm and myrrh, who were making their way down to Egypt on a trade mission.

Judah, the fourth brother, said to the others: 'What shall we gain if we kill our brother and conceal his death? Why not sell him to the Ishmaelites and not lay our hands on him; after all, he is our brother, our own flesh and blood.' The rest of the brothers, apart from Reuben, who was not present at that precise moment, agreed. They pulled Joseph out of the pit and sold him to the merchants for twenty shekels of silver.

'What can I do now?' Reuben asked when he returned and found that Joseph was missing. The remaining brothers were equal to the situation. They slaughtered a goat and dipped Joseph's robe in the animal's blood before taking it home to Jacob, who recognised it. 'It is my son's robe,' he said. 'Some wild beast has devoured him. Joseph has surely been torn to pieces.' Jacob wept for the best-loved son who, unknown to him, was on his way to Egypt, where the Ishmaelite merchants sold him to Potiphar, one of Pharaoh's officials, the captain of the guard.

Chapter 38 of the Book of Genesis is devoted to an account of Judah's marriage and the events that led to the founding of the Messianic line of King David, but with the next chapter we are back with Joseph in Egypt where, at the start, everything went well with him. Potiphar found him to be a faithful servant and entrusted to his care everything he owned. However, Joseph was not only efficient, but handsome, and after a while Potiphar's wife took notice of him and said: 'Come to bed with me.' Joseph rejected her invitation. 'Think of my master,' he told her. 'With me in charge, he does not concern' himself with anything in the house; everything he owns he has entrusted to my care. No one is greater in this house than I am. My master has withheld nothing from me except you, because you are his wife. How then could I do such a wicked thing and sin against God?'

Potiphar's wife was not prepared to take no for an answer. She continued to entreat Joseph to take her to bed and he continued to refuse. Eventually there came a day when he found himself alone in the house with her. She caught him by the cloak and pleaded again: 'Come. and lie with me,' but Joseph still refused and ran out of the house, leaving his cloak in her hand. Then followed what we may assume was not the first, and certainly was not the last, case of revengeful behaviour by a woman scorned.

Potiphar's wife told her other servants that Joseph had attacked her and had run out of the house when she screamed. She kept his cloak and repeated the same story to her husband when he arrived home: 'That Hebrew slave you brought us came to me to make a mockery of me, but as soon as I screamed for help he left his cloak in my hand and ran out of the house.' Potiphar, who believed her, was understandably outraged and promptly incarcerated Joseph in the jail where all the king's prisoners were kept.

Joseph proved such a model prisoner that he was soon running the internal affairs of the prison, much as he had run Potiphar's home. It was thus that he met Pharaoh's chief cupbearer and chief baker when they gave offence to the king and found themselves locked up in the same prison. After they had been there for some time, each had a disturbing dream. They looked dejected when Joseph came upon them the next morning. 'Why do you look so downcast today?' he asked.

'We both had dreams, but there is no one to interpret them,' they explained.

Joseph answered: 'Does not interpretation belong to God? Tell me your dreams.'

The chief cupbearer said: 'In my dream I saw a vine in front of me, and on the vine were three branches. As soon as it budded, it blossomed, and its clusters ripened into grapes. I had Pharaoh's cup in my hand, and I took the grapes, squeezed them into Pharaoh's cup and put the cup in his hand.'

'This is what it means,' Joseph told him. 'The three branches are three days. Within three days Pharaoh will raise your head and restore you to your position, and you will put Pharaoh's cup in his hand, just as you used to do when you were his cupbearer. But when all goes well with you, remember me and show me kindness; bring my case to Pharaoh's notice and get me out of this prison. For I was forcibly carried off from the land of the Hebrews, and even here I have done nothing to deserve being put in this dungeon.'

The chief baker then recounted his dream: 'On my head were three baskets of white bread. In the top basket were all kinds of baked goods for Pharaoh, but the birds were eating them out of the basket on my head.'

Joseph's interpretation of this second dream was less encouraging. 'This is what it means,' he said. 'The three baskets are three days. Within three days Pharaoh will behead you and hang your body on a tree. And the birds will eat away your flesh.'

The third day was Pharaoh's birthday and, as Joseph had predicted, he restored the cupbearer to his former position as part of the festivities, but, as Joseph had also foretold, the chief baker was executed. In a commonplace act of ingratitude, however, the cupbearer forgot to mention Joseph to Pharaoh. He did not think of him until two years later when Pharaoh himself had two mysterious dreams that none of the magicians or wise men of Egypt could interpret for him. Reminded by these circumstances of his own earlier predicament, the cupbearer said to Pharaoh: 'Pharaoh was once angry with his servants, and he imprisoned me and the chief baker. Each of us had a dream the same night, and each needed its own interpretation. Now a young servant was there with us, a servant of the captain of the guard. We told him our dreams, and he interpreted them for us, giving each man the interpretation of his dream. And things turned out exactly as he had interpreted them to us . . .'

Pharaoh sent at once for Joseph who, as soon as he had shaved and changed his clothes, presented himself before the king. Pharaoh explained: 'I have had a dream, and no one can interpret it. I have heard it said that you can understand and interpret dreams.'

'I cannot do it, but God will give Pharaoh the answer he desires,' Joseph replied.

'In my dream I was standing on the bank of the Nile when out of the river there came seven cows, fat and sleek, and they grazed among the reeds,' Pharaoh went on. 'After them appeared seven other cows

—scrawny and very gaunt and lean. These lean, gaunt cows ate up the seven fat ones. But even after they ate them no one could tell that they had done so; they looked as gaunt as before. In my dreams I also saw seven ears of corn, full and good, growing on a single stalk. After them, seven other ears sprouted—withered and thin and blighted by the east wind. The thin ears swallowed up the seven good ears. I told this to the magicians, but none could explain it to me.'

'The dreams of Pharaoh are one and the same,' Joseph told the king. 'God has told Pharaoh what he is about to do. The seven good cows are seven years, and the seven good ears of corn are seven years. The seven lean, gaunt cows are seven years, and so are the worthless ears of corn blighted by the east wind. Seven years of plenty are coming throughout the land of Egypt, but seven years of famine will follow them. Then all the abundance in Egypt will be forgotten, and the famine will ravage the land. Now, let Pharaoh look for a shrewd and wise man and put him in charge of the country. Let Pharaoh appoint commissioners to take a fifth of the harvest of Egypt during the seven years of abundance. They should store up the grain under the authority of Pharaoh, to be kept in the cities for food.'

To Pharaoh and all his officials the plan seemed a sensible one, and he said to Joseph: 'Since a god has made all this known to you, there is no one so shrewd and wise as you. You shall be in charge of my household, and all my people are to submit to your orders. Only in respect of the throne shall I be greater than you.'

Pharaoh took the signet ring from his own hand and placed it on Joseph's finger. He also dressed him in robes of fine linen, put a gold chain around his neck and arranged for Joseph to ride in a chariot as his second-in-command. Men shouted before him: 'Bow the knee.' In addition, the king gave him an Egyptian name, Zaphnath-pa-a-neah, as well as an Egyptian wife, Asenath, daughter of Potipherah, the priest of On (Heliopolis), the centre in Lower Egypt of the worship of the sun-god Re.

Joseph was thirty when he entered Pharaoh's service and, during the seven good years, he travelled throughout Egypt, storing grain against the lean years to come. He also became the father of two sons, Manasseh and Ephraim. Then came the years of predicted famine, which affected many countries, including Canaan, where Jacob said to his sons: 'I have heard that there is corn in Egypt. Go down there and buy some so that we don't starve.' The brothers set off, leaving behind only Benjamin, a second child who had been born to Rachel after Joseph. Joseph recognised his brothers as soon as he saw them, but he concealed his identity and spoke harshly to them through an interpreter. 'Where do you come from?' he asked.

'From the land of Canaan to buy food,' they replied.

'You are spies,' said Joseph. 'You have come to spy out the weaknesses of our defences.'

The brothers denied the charge and explained: 'Your servants were twelve brothers, the sons of one man who lives in the land of Canaan. The youngest is now with our father in Canaan, and one is no more.'

Although he knew their words to be true, except that in his own case he was still very much alive, Joseph locked the brothers up for three days. At the end of that time he said to them: 'If you are honest men, let one of your brothers stay here in prison while the rest of you take corn back to your starving households. But you must bring your youngest brother to me so that your words may be verified and that you may not die. Unless your youngest brother comes here, as Pharaoh lives you will not leave this place.'

Simeon was the brother chosen to stay behind. Joseph had the sacks of the others filled with grain, but he refused to let them pay for it and, without their knowledge, placed the silver in their sacks as well. He also gave them provisions for their journey, and they set out for Canaan with their laden donkeys. When they arrived home and their father, Jacob, heard the story of their adventures, he was at first reluctant to let them return to Egypt with Benjamin, who had clearly replaced Joseph as his favourite son. 'My son will not go down there with you,' he said. 'Joseph is dead and he is the only one left. If harm comes to him you will bring my grey hairs down to the grave in sorrow.'

The famine continued to rage, however, and, when all the grain was gone, Jacob changed his mind. 'If it must be done, then do this,' he said. 'Take some of the produce for which our country is famous—a little balm and a little honey, some spices and myrrh, some pistachio nuts and almonds—and take them with you as a gift. Take double the amount of silver with you, for you must return the silver that was put back in the mouths of your sacks. Perhaps it was a mistake. Take your other brother also and go back to the man at once. And may God Almighty grant you mercy before the man so that he will let your other brother (Simeon) and Benjamin come back with you.'

When the brothers arrived in Egypt for the second time and Joseph saw Benjamin with them, he said to his steward: 'Take these men to my house and slaughter an animal. They are to eat with me at noon.' At the house they were given water to wash their feet and fodder for their donkeys, and afterwards they prepared their gifts in readiness for Joseph's appearance. Once the gifts had been presented, Joseph asked: 'How is your aged father you told me about? Is he still living?'

They answered: 'Your servant our father is still alive and well.'

Turning to Benjamin, Joseph inquired: 'Is this your youngest brother, the one you told me about?' and added: 'God be gracious to you, my son.' Deeply moved at the sight of his own mother's son whom he had not seen for so many years, Joseph hurried out to his own private room to weep. Later, after he had washed his face, he came out and, controlling himself, said: 'Serve the food.' In terms of the seating arrangements, the meal could not be described as exactly convivial. Joseph ate alone and the Egyptians present ate apart from the brothers 'because Egyptians could not eat with Hebrews, for that is detestable to Egyptians'.

By the time the brothers were ready to depart, Joseph had hatched a plot designed to ensure that Benjamin would have to stay behind in Egypt. He told his steward: 'Fill the men's sacks with as much food as they can carry, and put each man's silver in the mouth of his sack. Then put my goblet, the silver one, at the top of the youngest one's sack.' The brothers had barely started out for Canaan again when Joseph sent his steward in pursuit, armed with the accusation that one of them had stolen his silver cup. They denied the theft, but, when the goblet was found in Benjamin's sack, they reloaded their donkeys and returned to the city to be confronted by Joseph. 'What can we say?' asked Judah despairingly. 'How can we prove our innocence? We are now our lord's slaves—we ourselves as well as the one who was found with the goblet.'

Joseph replied that he would not be so harsh: 'Only the one found with the goblet will become my slave. The rest of you can go back to your father in peace.'

Judah pleaded with him to change his mind, explaining: 'My father said to us: "You know that my wife bore me two sons. One of them left me and I said: 'He has surely been torn to pieces.' If you take this one, too, from me and harm comes to him, you will bring my grey hairs down to the grave in sorrow." Please let your servant remain here as my lord's slave in place of the boy, and let the boy return with his brothers.'

Joseph was so touched by this voluntary act of self-sacrifice that he decided to reveal himself at last to his brothers. 'Come close to me,' he said, and when they had approached him went on: 'I am your brother Joseph, the one you sold into Egypt. And now, do not be distressed and do not be angry with yourselves for selling me here, because it was God who sent me ahead of you to save lives . . .

'So it was not you who sent me here, but God. He has made me a father to Pharaoh, lord over all his household and ruler of all Egypt. Now hurry back to my father and tell him: "This is what your son Joseph says: 'God has made me lord of all Egypt. Come down to me; don't delay. You shall live in the region of Goshen[1] and be near me—you, your sons and grandsons, your flocks and herds, and all you have. I shall provide for you there, because five years of famine are still to come.'"'

When Pharaoh heard that Joseph's brothers were in Egypt, he said to him: 'Tell your brothers: "Load your animals and go back to Canaan, and bring your father and your families back to me. I shall give you the best land in Egypt." You are also directed to tell them: "Take some wagons from Egypt for your children and your wives, and get your father and come."'

Jacob (or Israel, to use the new name he had been given so many years before) was stunned to hear that his long-lost son, Joseph, was still alive, and did not really believe it until he had heard all the details and seen the carts that Pharaoh had sent. He gathered together his entire family, nearly seventy souls in all, and they set out for Egypt. Joseph drove out in his chariot to meet them, and, after an emotional reunion, Jacob said to him: 'Now I am ready to die, since I have seen for myself that you are still alive.'

Joseph settled all his family in the Goshen district of Ramses and introduced his father and five of his brothers to Pharaoh, who told Joseph: 'If you know of any capable men among them, make them chief herdsmen over my cattle.' They had lived there for seventeen years when Jacob, who felt that the time of his death was approaching, sent for Joseph and said to him: 'Do not bury me in Egypt, but when I

[1] In the eastern delta.

die carry me out of Egypt and bury me where my forefathers are buried.'

'I shall do as you say,' Joseph promised.

'Swear to me,' his father said. Joseph swore to him.

Some time later, Joseph learned that his father was ill and went to visit him, accompanied by his own two sons, Manasseh and Ephraim. There then followed another curious incident. The two sons went close to their grandfather to receive his blessing, Ephraim, the younger, standing on the right in reach of his left hand, and Manasseh, the elder, standing on the left in reach of his right hand. However, Jacob crossed his hands and put his right hand on Ephraim's head. Joseph was displeased by this departure from normal custom, so he took hold of his father's right hand to move it from Ephraim's head to Manasseh's, saying: 'This one is the elder. Put your right hand on his head.' Jacob refused, however, saying: 'I know, my son, I know. He, too, will become a great people, and he, too, will become great. Nevertheless, his younger brother will be greater than he, and his descendants will be a whole nation in themselves.' The Old Testament offers no explanation for this strange exchange, the meaning of Jacob's words or whether his promise was ever fulfilled.

When Jacob eventually died, Joseph gave orders for him to be embalmed and, after seventy days of mourning, asked permission to take his father's body back to Canaan for burial. Pharaoh granted his request. It was an impressive caravan that set out for Canaan with all the adults from Joseph's and his brothers' families, all the dignitaries of Egypt, chariots and horsemen. On their subsequent return to Egypt, however, Joseph's brothers feared that, with their father dead, Joseph would take revenge on them for selling him into slavery. As a precaution, they sent him a message saying: 'Your father left these instructions before he died. This is what you are to say to Joseph: "I ask you to forgive your brothers' crime: I know they did you harm."' Joseph gave them his reassurance. 'Don't be afraid,' he told them. 'Am I in place of God? You intended to harm me, but God meant to bring good out of it, to accomplish what is now being done, the saving of many lives. So don't be afraid. I shall provide for you and your children.'

Immediately after that, we come to an account of Joseph's own death. There is no indication of how much time had elapsed since the death of his father, but we are told that he 'saw the third generation of

Ephraim's children. Also the children of Makir, son of Manasseh, were placed at birth on Joseph's knees.' Before he died, Joseph foretold the Exodus: 'But God will not fail to come to your aid and take you up out of this land to the land he promised on oath to Abraham, Isaac and Jacob.' Joseph also made the sons of Israel themselves swear an oath: 'When God comes to your aid, you must take my bones with you from here.'

The Book of Genesis ends with his death: 'So Joseph died at the age of a hundred and ten. And after they embalmed him he was laid in a coffin in Egypt.'

To summarise the views accepted by scholars about the way the Joseph story has come down to us, there was an original narration, which was put down in writing about the ninth century BC and is thought to be the Judah–Israel version (J). About a century later there came a second story, believed to be the Reuben–Jacob version (E). The story of Joseph in the Book of Genesis comes mainly from these two sources (see also Book Two, Chapter Two). However, after returning from their Babylonian exile, the priests who arranged the sources made some additions of their own (P) that included Joseph's age (thirty) at the time he entered the service of Pharaoh, the number of the tribe of Israel who went down to join him in Egypt, the length of their sojourn and Joseph's request to be buried in Canaan. Then came the editor who, some time before the second century BC, took on the task of making one story from these three sources and, furthermore, was responsible for the section dealing with Joseph's death and his request to be re-buried in Canaan.

Chapter 5

JOSEPH IN THE KORAN

It was another descendant of Abraham—from his son Ismael (Ishmael), born of Sarah's Egyptian maid, Hagar—who, eighteen centuries after the Exodus, became the messenger of Islam. Muhammad, who was born in Mecca in the year AD 570, started his mission when he was about forty years of age, preaching to Arab idolators the true faith, Islam, the monotheistic *Hanif*[1] religion of his remote ancestor. Muhammad had completed delivering the Koran, Islam's holy book, shortly before his death in the year 632. The Koran, believed by Muslims to be the inspired word of God, was first written on date leaves and stone as well as being memorised by some of Muhammad's followers. Later it was collected by Abu Bakr, the first caliph (civil and religious ruler) after Muhammad's death. Finally it was compiled into one book by Uthman, the third caliph, about ten years later.

The Koran accepts the biblical story of the Creation and agrees with both the Old and New Testaments in the main about the stories of the patriarchs and the prophets. However, while identifying the one God revealed to Moses as Allah, the Koran regards Jesus as the Messiah, created of the Holy Spirit although not the son of God. Furthermore, although the Koran springs from the same fountain as the Bible, it does disagree with the latter in some other respects. In general, the stories in the Koran lack many of the details found in the Bible, especially those dealing with figures, dates, proper nouns and locations. On the other hand, in some cases we find extra information about biblical characters that is not to be found in the Bible itself. In all, the story of Joseph in the Koran might be said to strike a more spiritual, and less historical, note.

[1] *Hanif* is the Islamic word for someone who believes in one God, but is not a Jew, a Christian or a worshipper of idols.

In the Koran, the whole of Sura (Chapter) XII is devoted to the story of Yussuf (Joseph). The Koran story does not mention the name of any of the other brothers, whose number is indicated only by the fact that Joseph's second dream, as in the Bible, has eleven stars prostrating themselves before him:

> Behold, Joseph said
> To his father: 'O my father!
> I did see eleven stars
> And the sun and the moon;
> I saw them prostrate themselves
> To me!'

The name of Joseph's father is given only as Jacob and his sons are described only as being of 'the house of Jacob'. Jacob is never called Israel, nor are his children called *Bani Israel* (children of Israel), which is always used in the Koran to describe the followers of Moses. On hearing of Joseph's dreams, his father warns him:

> 'Relate not thy vision
> To thy brothers, lest they
> Concoct a plot against thee.'

It is already too late, however. The brothers' resentment has been aroused by the favouritism shown by their father:

> They said: 'Truly Joseph
> And his brother[1] are loved
> More by our father than we.'

The brothers plan to kill Joseph, but once again there is a good brother who argues against it:

> Said one of them: 'Slay not
> Joseph, but if ye must
> Do something, throw him down
> To the bottom of the well.'

Joseph, according to the Koran story, appears to have been still only a child at the time, because the brothers persuade Jacob to allow

---

[1] This must clearly be a reference to Benjamin, the second son born to Jacob's first love, Rachel.

Joseph out 'to play' with them, promising to take good care of him.
However, they throw him into a well, sell him to the caravan (whose
origins are not identified), stain Joseph's shirt with false blood and
return to their father with a similar story to that in the Bible:

> They said: 'O our father!
> We went racing with one another,
> And left Joseph with our things:
> And the wolf devoured him.'

The Egyptian who bought Joseph is identified only by the title *Al
Aziz*, which means 'the prince' or vizier, the title that would be given to
Joseph himself later. The indications are that he reached maturity in
his master's house and received some learning in the process. The story
of the attempted seduction that then follows is given in some detail:

> But she, in whose house
> He was, sought to seduce him
> From his (true) self; she fastened
> The doors, and said:
> 'Now come, thou (dear one)!'
> He said: 'Allah forbid!
> Truly (thy husband) is
> My lord! He made
> My sojourn agreeable!
> Truly to no good
> Come those who do wrong!'

Joseph tried to make his escape, pursued by his master's wife, who
tore his shirt from the back, and, on opening the door, Joseph found
his master standing outside it. The wife promptly said:

> 'What is the (fitting) punishment
> For one who formed
> An evil design against
> Thy wife, but prison
> Or a grievous chastisement?'

> He (Joseph) said: 'It was she
> That sought to seduce me—
> From my (true) self.' And one
> Of her household saw (this)

And bore witness, (thus):—
'If it be that his shirt
Is rent from the front, then
Is her tale true,
And he is a liar!

'But if it be that his shirt
Is torn from the back,
Then is she the liar,
And he is telling the truth!'

On seeing that Joseph's shirt was torn from the back, his master told him to ignore what had happened and suggested that his wife should ask forgiveness for her sin because it was all her fault. The wife was not yet finished with Joseph, however. When she heard that women in the city were gossiping about her attempt to seduce him:

She sent for them
And prepared a banquet
For them: she gave
Each of them a knife;
And she said (to Joseph),
'Come out before them.'
When they saw him,
They did extol him,
And (in their amazement)
Cut their hands; they said
'Allah preserve us! No mortal
Is this! This is none other
Than a noble angel!'

She (the wife) said: 'There before you
Is the man about whom
Ye did blame me!'

At the same time, she made it clear that her efforts to seduce Joseph were not yet over, and, although there was no evidence to justify his action, her husband eventually put Joseph into prison as a precautionary measure. There, as in the Old Testament story, he encounters the chief cupbearer and chief baker and interprets their dreams with the same consequences, happy for one, dire for the other. Again, as in the Bible, the cupbearer forgets to put in a plea with Pharaoh on Joseph's behalf.

The name 'Pharaoh' does not actually appear in Sura XII: nor is the name of the Egyptian ruler given. The only title mentioned for the ruler is 'king', which occurs three times. The king has the same dreams about the fat and lean cows and the green-eared and withered corn, but they come to him 'some years' rather than two years after the incidents involving the cupbearer and baker, and, in the Koran, the king does not summon Joseph to his presence, but sends his attendants to see him. It is only after he has given his interpretation of the dreams that Joseph is brought to the palace, and then only after he has refused release from prison until he has been cleared of the false charge of attempted seduction. Questioned by the king, the wife of *Al Aziz* admits that it was she who had sought to seduce Joseph, but adds:

> 'He is indeed of those
> Who are (ever) true (and virtuous).'

According to the Koran account, it was not the king who offered Joseph a Royal appointment, but Joseph who asked for one:

> (Joseph) said: 'Set me
> Over the store-houses
> Of the land: I will
> Indeed guard them,
> As one that knows
> Their importance.'

The Koran account makes no mention of Joseph being given an Egyptian name or an Egyptian wife, but, as in the Old Testament, his brothers arrive to buy food, and once he has provided it he says:

> 'Bring unto me a brother
> Ye have, of the same father
> As yourselves (but a different mother):
>
> Now if ye bring him not
> To me, ye shall have
> No measure (of corn) from me,
> Nor shall ye (even) come
> Near me.'

Although Joseph had recognised his brothers, they were not aware of his identity at this time. They returned home to Jacob with the news that they would not be given any more opportunities to buy corn in Egypt unless they brought their younger brother with them. Initially, Jacob was reluctant to give permission, remembering what had happened in the past. He asked:

> 'Shall I trust you
> With him with any result
> Other than when I trusted you
> With his brother aforetime?'

Eventually, however, he agreed to let his youngest son accompany them back to Egypt on condition that they swore 'a solemn oath to me, in Allah's name, that ye will be sure to bring him back to me unless ye are yourselves hemmed in (and made powerless).' Jacob also had some advice for them about how to enter the Egyptian city when they reached it again: 'Enter not all by one gate: enter ye by different gates.'

When the brothers arrived in Egypt for the second time, Joseph invited the youngest of them to stay with him and revealed to him, but not the others, that they were true brothers, born of the same mother and father. The Koran then gives a similar account of the ruse with the 'stolen' drinking cup to keep the younger brother in Egypt. In the Koran story, however, it is the elder brother, whose name we are not told, who remains in Egypt as well while the rest of the party return to break their bad news to Jacob.

Jacob, who has never really believed that Joseph died on the distant day when his brothers took him out to play, sends them back to Egypt yet a third time, on this occasion to seek Joseph. On this third visit they finally recognise Joseph, who admits his identity and tells them to fetch their father and all their relations and come down to Egypt to live:

> Then when they entered
> The presence of Joseph,
> He provided a home
> For his parents with himself,
> And said: 'Enter ye
> Egypt (all) in safety
> If it pleases Allah.'

And he raised his parents[1]
High on the throne,
And they fell down in prostration
(All) before him. He said:
'O my father! This is
The fulfilment of my vision
Of old! Allah hath made it
Come true. He was indeed
Good to me when He
Took me out of prison
And brought you (all here)
Out of the desert,
(Even) after Satan had sown
Enmity between me and my brothers.'

Joseph's story in the Koran is not intended, as in the Bible, to serve as a link between the patriarchal and the Exodus narrations. The accounts of the birth of Moses, the Oppression and the Exodus are scattered through different Suras and do not have a direct connection with the Joseph story. There are differences between the two narrations, some of which I have already indicated. Others exist. The Koran, for instance, suggests that Joseph's brothers made their journeys to and from Egypt by camel rather than by donkey, and the Koran story virtually stops at the point where Joseph speaks of the fulfilment of his vision of old. No mention is made of the settlement of Jacob's descendants in Egypt, the agrarian reforms carried out by Joseph that are described at some length in the latter pages of the Book of Genesis, or the death of either Jacob or Joseph. Yet for the greater part these two versions of the Joseph story, from different sources but both held to be the inspired word of God, are identical. The Koran account includes two main sections—Joseph's dream and how it was eventually fulfilled, which seems to agree with the biblical (E) source; and the relationship between Joseph and his master's wife, reported in greater detail than in the Bible, which is generally regarded as belonging to the biblical (J) source. No section can be found that would agree with either the priestly source (P) or the later additions that are

[1] This verse (100) in the Koran indicates that Joseph's mother was still alive at the time the tribe of Israel went down to live in Egypt. Some biblical scholars also believe this to be the case (A Study of the Biblical Story of Joseph, Donald B. Redford).

thought to be the work of the biblical editor. This reinforces the conviction that the original Joseph story was included in the first two sources, (J) and (E), before the biblical editor gave it its final shape, adding his own interpretation.

Chapter 6

THE TIME OF YUYA

From the point of view of Egyptian history, the biblical Joseph is a misty figure. No record of the name Joseph or that of any other members of his family has been found, and there is, to date, only one recorded discovery of the name Israel. In contrast, we know a good deal, from his tomb and other sources, about Yuya—when he was alive, his family, the posts he held.

I believe that Tuthmosis IV (c.1413–1405 BC) was the Pharaoh who appointed Yuya to the post of vizier. Tuthmosis IV seems to have been an Egyptian counterpart of Jacob and Joseph, a dreamer (see Chapter 9). We are told that one day, as a young prince, he went hunting in his chariot near the pyramids. At noon, when the sun was at its highest, he rested in the shadow of the Sphinx and fell asleep. The gigantic Sphinx was at that time more than half buried, with only its head visible above the sand. In his sleep, the prince had a vision in which he was addressed by Harmakhis, the sun-god with whom the Sphinx was identified, who said: 'Behold me, gaze on me, O my son Tuthmosis, for I, thy father Harmakhis-Khopri-Tumu, grant thee sovereignty over the Two Lands, in the South and the North, and thou shalt wear both the white and the red crowns of the throne of Sibu, the sovereign possessing the earth in its length and breadth. The flashing eye of the lord of all shall cause to rain on thee the possessions of Egypt. Vast tribute from all foreign countries, and a long life for many years as one chosen by the Sun, for my countenance is thine, my heart is thine, no other than thyself is mine. Now I am covered by the sand of the mountain on which I rest, and have given thee this prize that thou mayest do for me what my heart desires, for I know thou art my son, my defender; draw nigh, I am with thee, I am thy well-beloved father.'[1] The prince took this encounter as a covenant between him and the god: he will inherit

[1] *The Struggle of the Nations*, Gaston Maspero.

the kingdom if he clears the sand from the Sphinx. Immediately upon his accession to the throne, Tuthmosis IV hastened to fulfil his part of the covenant and, in order to preserve the memory of his action, recorded its details on a stele that is still to be found against the breast of the Sphinx between its forelegs.

Yuya, who had married an Egyptian woman named Tuya, possibly of Royal blood (see also Book Two, Chapter Three), continued to serve as vizier when Tuthmosis IV died and was succeeded by his son, Amenhotep III (c.1405–1367 BC). Amenhotep III, who was only twelve years of age at the time, broke with Egyptian tradition by marrying first his sister, Sitamun, and then Yuya's daughter, Tiye—herself thought to have been only about eight—and making her rather than Sitamun his Great Royal Wife (queen).

The first we heard of Yuya in modern times was with the discovery during the second half of the last century of five commemorative scarabs issued by Amenhotep III. They reported: 1) The king's marriage to Tiye, 2) His wild-cattle hunt, 3) The record of ten years'

CHRONOLOGY OF THE EIGHTEENTH DYNASTY[1]

	Highest Dated	Conjectural Dates BC
Ahmosis	22	1575–1550
Amenhotep I	21	1550–1528
Tuthmosis I	4 or 9	1528–1510
Tuthmosis II	18	1510–1490
Hatshepsut	20 or 22	1490–1468
Tuthmosis III	54	1490–1436
Amenhotep II	23	1436–1413
Tuthmosis IV	8 or 9	1413–1405
Amenhotep III	38 or 39	1405–1367
Amenhotep IV (Akhnaten)	17	1367–1350
Semenkhkare	3	1350–1347
Tutankhamun	9	1347–1339
Aye	4	1339–1335
Horemheb	27 or 28	1335–1308

[1] Egypt of the Pharaohs, Alan Gardiner.

lion-hunting, 4) His marriage to Princess Kirgipa,[1] 5) The construction of a pleasure lake for Queen Tiye. Only three of the five scarabs—recording his wild cattle hunt (Year 2: 1404 or 1403 BC), the marriage to Princess Kirgipa (Year 10: 1396 or 1395 BC) and the construction of the pleasure lake (Year 11: 1395 or 1394 BC)—bear a date.

Yuya's name, as well as that of his wife, was first mentioned in the marriage scarab of his daughter: 'Live . . . King Amenhotep (III), who is given life, (and) the Great King's-Wife Tiye, who liveth. The name of her father is Yuya, the name of her mother is Tuya. She is the wife of a mighty king whose southern boundary is as far as Karoy and northern as far as Naharin.'[2] Although this scarab is not dated, Amenhotep III must already have been married to Tiye, whose name appears again on the wild-cattle hunt scarab, which dates from the second year of his reign and bears the inscription: 'Year 2 under the majesty of King Amenhotep (III) given life, and the Great King's-Wife Tiye, living like Re.' The name of Tiye, in fact, appears on all five scarabs and those of Yuya and Tuya on the Kirgipa marriage scarab as well as that of their daughter: '. . . the Son of Re, Amenhotep (III), Ruler of Thebes, who is granted life; (and) the Great King's-Wife, Tiye, who liveth; the name of whose father was Yuya, the name of whose mother was Tuya. Marvels brought to his majesty . . . Kirgipa, the daughter of the chief of Naharin, Satirna; (and) the chief of her harem-ladies, (viz.) 317 persons.'

It is interesting in the context of the scarabs to read Breasted's comments in *Ancient Records of Egypt, II*: 'The origin of the powerful Tiye is obscure; Maspero thinks her a native Egyptian, and this is the most probable conclusion, but the persistent publication of the names of her untitled parents on these and other scarabs is in that case remarkable, although paralleled by scarabs of the Thirteenth Dynasty. This difficulty is, however, not relieved by supposing her of foreign birth. It is incredible that anyone could identify her with Kirgipa, on whose marriage scarab she already appears in the titulary as queen. She is the first queen who is thus recognised by the regular insertion of

[1] The princess was a Mitannian, from the upper part of modern Iraq where Gilkhipa, a modern version of her name, is still common.

[2] *Ancient Records of Egypt, II*, John Henry Breasted. Copies of this scarab were also found by Flinders Petrie in Palestine. The mention of Karoy and Naharin basically establishes Amenhotep III's kingdom as stretching from the Nile to the Euphrates.

Canopic boxes of Yuya *(left)* and Tuya, from their tomb. Each divided into four compartments, they held the canopic vases containing the mummified viscera of the dead. *(Below)* Canopic jar with mummified liver, surmounted by a cartonnage mask. *Photos: Cairo Museum.*

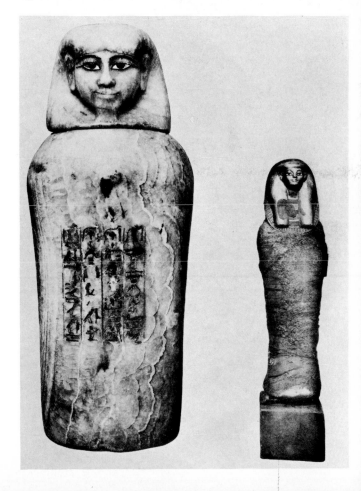

Painted wooden boxes belonging to Yuya. They contained quantities of *ushabti*, small figures resembling the mummy of the deceased, whose role was to act as substitute for him in the underworld. *Photo: Cairo Museum*

Yuya's necklace of large gold and lapis lazuli beads. This had been broken by the early tomb robber and was found, forgotten, under the mummy's neck. Could this have been the gold chain given to him by Pharaoh? *Photo: Cairo Museum*

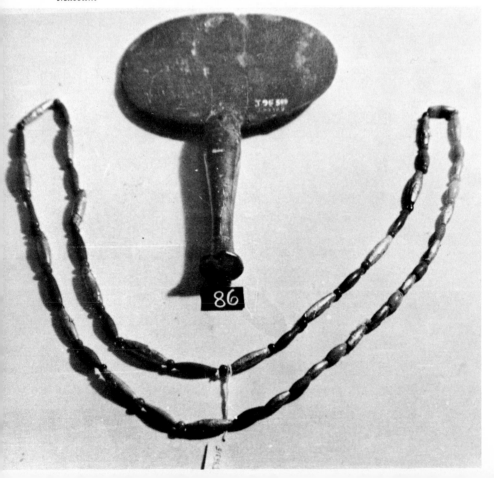

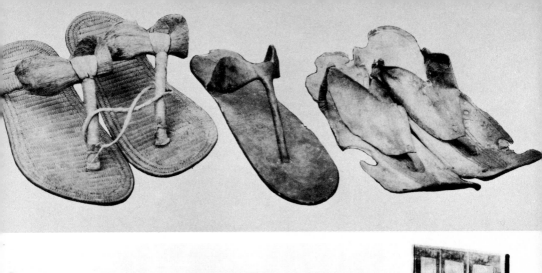

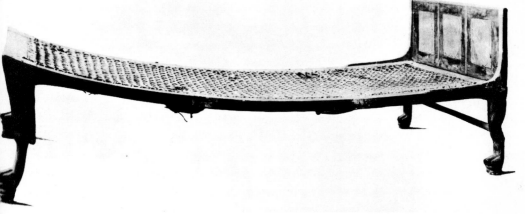

(Top) Papyrus and leather sandals from the
tomb. *Photo: Cairo Museum*

(Above) Bed with panelled headpiece, one of
two found in the tomb. *Photo: Cairo Museum*

(Right) Tuthmosis III from Karnak. Could he
have been the father of Isaac? *Photo: Cairo
Museum*

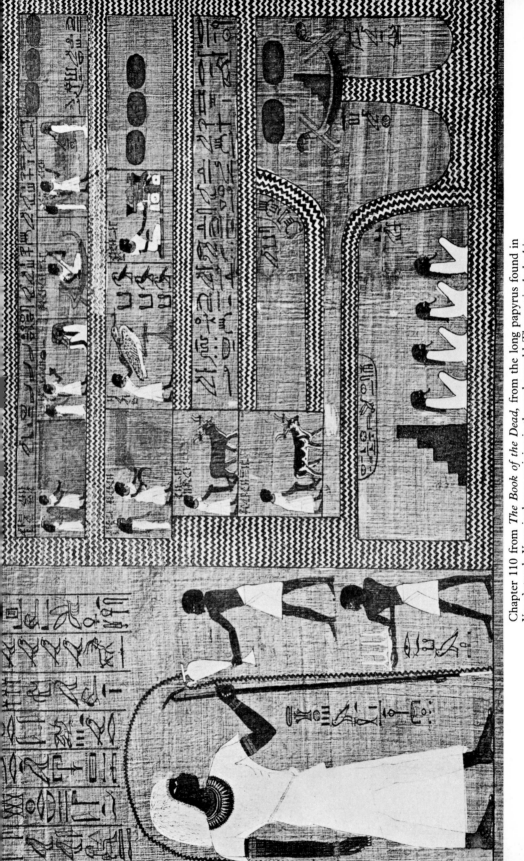

Chapter 110 from *The Book of the Dead*, from the long papyrus found in Yuya's tomb. Yuya is shown arriving in the underworld. The text includes his many titles: 'Prince, Bearer of the seal (ring) of the King of Lower Egypt, ...

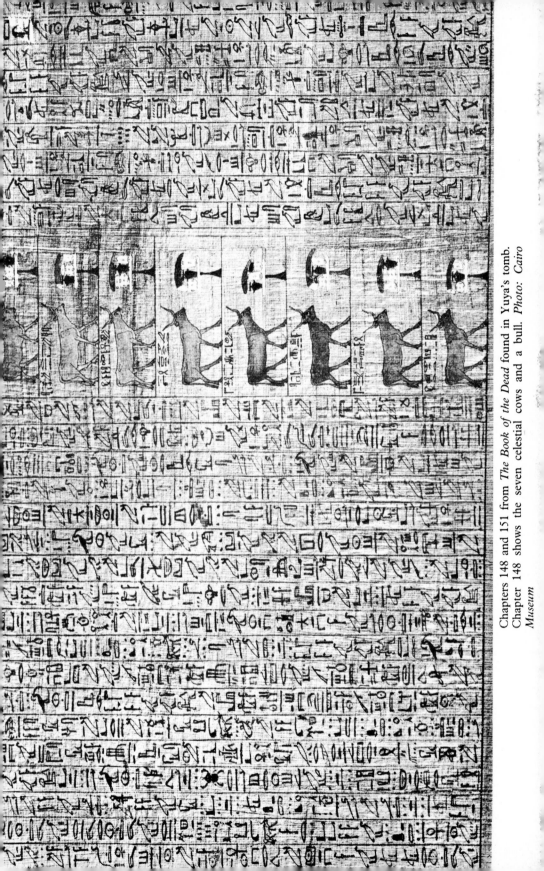

Chapters 148 and 151 from *The Book of the Dead* found in Yuya's tomb. Chapter 148 shows the seven celestial cows and a bull. *Photo: Cairo Museum*

(Above) Tuthmosis IV and his mother Tia, found at Karnak. *Photo: Cairo Museum*

(Left) The Dream Stele of Tuthmosis IV, which he placed between the forelegs of the Sphinx as a record of his covenant with the sun-god, with whom the Sphinx was identified. It is still there today. *Photo: Cairo Museum*

Colossi of Amenhotep III and his Queen Tiye from the royal funerary temple west of Thebes. *Photo: Cairo Museum*

The head of Amenhotep III from Thebes. *Photo: British Museum*

The head of Queen Tiye, found by Petrie in the temple of Serabet el-Khadem in Sinai. *Photo: Cairo Museum*

her name in the titulary. The innovation was continued by Amenhotep
IV, who inserted his queen's name in the same way. His ephemeral
successors show the same inclination, and the whole period from the
time of Amenhotep III to the close of the Eighteenth Dynasty is
characterised by the mention and prominent representation of the
queens on all state occasions, in such a manner as is never found later.'

Further evidence that Yuya lived during this period, and died during
his son-in-law's reign, is provided by the objects found in his tomb
with Amenhotep III's name on them—the jewel-box, the chest and the
alabaster vase—and the absence of any gifts from the ruler who
succeeded him, Akhnaten. When it comes to trying to establish the
precise year of his death, however, we encounter a major difficulty.
There is no date of any kind to be found among the inscriptions on
Yuya's funerary furniture; nor is there any record of a name or an
event that can help us to establish the year. In fact, the latest precise
date we have for Yuya being alive is the scarab recording the construction of the pleasure lake in the eleventh year of Amenhotep III's reign.[1]
Nevertheless, it is possible to make some further reasonable deduc-
tions about his life.

One of the most significant pieces of evidence is the three chairs,
found in his tomb, that belonged to Princess Sitamun. The variations
in the height, width and depth of the chairs suggest that they were
made for the princess at three different stages of her growing up:

	Height	Width	Depth
First chair	595mm	400mm	370mm
Second chair	615mm	380mm	410mm
Third chair	770mm	520mm	540mm

The first chair has no inscription, but has scenes representing the
cat goddess Bes, dancing with her tambourine between two lion-
headed figures of Tueris, the hippopotamus goddess, on the back.
The second chair has Bes and Tueris on the sides, plus a boat
containing Sitamun, offering a bouquet of lotus flowers to the seated
Queen Tiye, with a cat under the queen's chair and another princess
standing behind. Above the queen is her name inscribed inside a Royal
cartouche (an oval ring containing hieroglyphic names and titles)—

[1] The copy of this scarab in the Vatican is described by Rosellini, *Monumenti
Storici*.

'The Great Royal Wife, Tiye'—while, behind Sitamun, is her name, also written in a cartouche: 'Praised of the Lord of the Two Lands, Sitamun.' Only part of the inscription relating to the other princess in the scene can be read: 'The daughter of the king . . .' According to Theodore M. Davis, the dimensions of this second chair prove that it must have been made for a child, and, as the gold has been rubbed off and patched again in places, it is probable that the princess used it in her younger years. The third and largest of the chairs—which, according to James Quibell, who took part in the search, is sufficiently large to have been used by a grown person—has, on the inside of the back, a double scene of Sitamun, seated and receiving a necklace of gold from a maiden. Her name, this time without a cartouche, is written above her.

Scholars have identified Sitamun as the daughter of Amenhotep III and Tiye, and claim that the king married her. I believe, as I said earlier, that she was the infant sister, perhaps about three at the time, whom Amenhotep III married in order to inherit the throne. Tuthmosis IV is known to have had at least two sons, Amenemhet and Amenhotep, and four daughters, Tentamun, Amenipet, Tia and Sitamun. Amenemhet and Tentamun both died early and were buried with their father in his tomb. Sitamun was therefore still alive at the time of her father's death.

Her name appears along with that of Amenhotep III inside a cartouche on a kohl-tube that is in the Metropolitan Museum in New York as well as inside the cartouche on one of the three chairs. The inscription on the bright blue, glazed faience tube, which probably came from Sitamun's palace at the King's Malkata complex at Thebes, is one of the main reasons that have led scholars to take the view —mistaken in my opinion—that Sitamun was Amenhotep's daughter as well as his wife. It reads: *ntr nfr (nb m'at Re) s3t-nsw-ḥmt-nsw wrt (St Amn)*, which is translated as 'the good god *(Neb-maat-Re)*, king's daughter, king's great wife (Sit-Amun)'.[1] It is the reference to 'king's daughter' which has persuaded scholars that she was the daughter of Amenhotep III. However, as in many other cases when a princess or a queen is described as being the daughter of a king, the name of the king is not given. Why then the assumption that it was Amenhotep III rather than his father, Tuthmosis IV? Moreover, by claiming to be the 'king's

[1] *Akhnaten, Pharaoh of Egypt*, Cyril Aldred.

great wife', which was Tiye's title, Sitamun is challenging Tiye's position, reinforcing the idea that she was the heiress her brother married in order to inherit the throne.

The presence of the chairs also indicates that, after her father's early death, Sitamun was reared by Tuya and must have been *at least* about fifteen years of age—and the possessor of yet a fourth chair—when she gave these three chairs to be included in the funerary furniture. This, and the evidence of the scarabs, suggest that Yuya's death could not have occurred earlier than Year 12 or 13 (1393/2 or 1392/1 BC) of Amenhotep III's reign. This, of course, is not to say that it did not take place later in his son-in-law's reign, which lasted according to the conjectural dates (1405–1367 BC) for thirty-eight or thirty-nine years. Opinions differ in the matter. Arthur Weigall asserts—without giving any reason—in his book *The Life and Times of Akhnaten* that 'it must have been somewhere about the year 1390 BC that Tiye's father, Yuya, died; and Tuya soon followed him to the grave.' In contrast, Christiane Desroches-Noblecourt, the former curator of the Egyptian section of the Louvre Museum, makes the statement—again without giving any reason—in her book *Tutankhamen* that Yuya died in Year 31 (1374 or 1373 BC) of Amenhotep III's reign.

The situation is not made any clearer by the fact that we do not know how old Yuya was when he died. Until modern techniques are used to examine his mummy and some of the contents of his tomb, we have nothing to go on except the opinions of Sir Grafton Elliot Smith, the anatomist who conducted the initial examination, and Gaston Maspero, the Director-General of Cairo Museum at the time. Elliot Smith said, in a report published in James Quibell's book, *Catalogue général des antiquités du Musée du Caire*, in 1908, three years after the discovery of Yuya's tomb: 'The mummy of Yuaa is that of an old, white-haired man ... His hair, now stained yellow by embalming materials, was perfectly white at the time of his death ... The skin of the forehead, as well as that of the cheeks, is wrinkled. In attempting to determine the age that Yuaa had attained at the time of his death there is little to rely on beyond his general appearance, his white hair and wrinkled skin. If, on these slight grounds, we estimate his age as about sixty years, it must be understood that the mention of such a figure is little more than guesswork.' Gaston Maspero had been less cautious in the foreword he wrote to Theodore M. Davis's book, *The Tomb of Iouiya and Touiyou*, published a year earlier: 'Iouiya and Touyiyou

died at a fairly advanced age: their hairs are white, and the examination of their bodies does not contradict the verdict of their hair. It will
not be a mistake to state that they had reached an age over sixty. From
the relative position of the two sarcophagi in the tomb, it seems that
the husband was the first to die; but the material is lacking to decide
this question.'

Although Amenhotep III's name is the only king's name to be found in
Yuya's tomb, this should not be taken as signifying automatically that
it was Amenhotep III who first appointed Yuya as vizier and gave him
his many titles. The fact that the new king, just after acceding to the
throne, made Yuya's daughter his queen indicates that they must have
known each other well as children. This would have been possible only
if it was Tuthmosis IV who appointed Yuya to his post. Yuya's titles included Master of the Horse and Deputy of His Majesty in the Chariotry,
while Tuya was the king's 'ornament' *(khrt nsw)*, a post which might
be said to combine the duties of a modern butler and lady-in-waiting.
Yuya's titles and the position of his wife would have required them to
live in the Royal residence. In those circumstances we can understand
how the young prince grew up with Tiye, became enchanted with her
and made her his queen when he came to the throne.

If this is the correct interpretation, and we assume for the sake of
argument:

1   That Yuya was sixty when he died during the reign of his son-in-
law, Amenhotep III,
2   That, because of the evidence of the three chairs, he could not have
died before the Princess Sitamun was at least fifteen years of age, and
3   That Akhnaten served for a time as co-regent with his father and
Year 26 of Amenhotep III is the earliest date this co-regency could have
begun, then it follows:

That Yuya died at some time between 1393/2 and 1379/8 BC,

That he was born at some time between 1453/2 and 1439/38 BC.

Chapter 7

KINGS FROM THE DESERT

There are four cornerstones to the accepted theory that Joseph and the Israelites arrived in Egypt at the time of the Hyksos rulers and the Exodus took place more than four centuries later in the reign of Ramses II, the third king of the Nineteenth Dynasty:

1   The ethnic coincidence that the Hyksos were, like the Israelites, Asiatic shepherds,
2   The reference to the Israelites having settled at Goshen 'in the Ramses region', which is the only mention of a Pharaonic name in the Old Testament,
3   The 400-year stele, issued by Ramses II, which provided a link with Avaris, the Hyksos capital, and
4   The biblical statement that the sojourn in Egypt would last four hundred and thirty years.

These facts fit together so neatly in many respects that they have had an irresistible appeal for the majority of scholars, even if they also contain inherent inconsistencies that have resulted in some strange contortions of argument to try to explain such inconsistencies away. One major difficulty is that neither the Old Testament nor the Koran offers direct help in the sense that they at no time give any indication of the identity of Egypt's ruler when Joseph appeared on the scene. In the biblical story of Joseph, the Egyptian sovereign is referred to as 'the king', 'the king of Egypt', 'Pharaoh, the king of Egypt' but mainly simply as 'Pharaoh', which is a Hebrew loan word from the Egyptian $pr'3$ (Great House). Originally it designated the Royal palace, but it was later transferred to the government and later still, from the Eighteenth Dynasty, to the king himself as a permanent title (out of respect for the person of the king, it was the practice to avoid using his own name in speech). Nor does the biblical narration tell us the name of the capital city where Pharaoh resided in Joseph's time, an omission which does not make it any easier to relate the patriarch to a specific period of ancient Egypt.

The Koran is equally unhelpful in these respects. The koranic story of Joseph uses only the title *Al Malik* (the king). *Fir'awn* (Pharaoh) does not appear at all in Sura XII and is to be found in the Koran only as a proper name, *Al Fir'awn*, referring to the ruler at the time of Moses, the Oppression and the Exodus.

The situation is not made any easier by the fact that the Pentateuch's description of life under Pharaoh in Joseph's time is couched in such general terms that it could apply to almost any period in ancient Egypt except, as Eric Peet, the late Professor of Egyptology at Liverpool University, pointed out in his book *Egypt and the Old Testament*: 'The references to chariots do indeed indicate that the writer is describing a state of things not earlier than the Hyksos date, when the horse was first introduced into Egypt.'

It was Josephus, the Jewish historian, who first suggested, in his book *Contra Apionem*, written towards the end of the first century AD, that the Israelites' descent into Egypt and their Exodus took place during the Hyksos rule. Josephus, quoting Manetho, an Egyptian priest of the third century BC, gives us the following account of the appearance of the Hyksos rulers: 'Tutimaios. In his reign, for what cause I know not, a blast of God smote us; and unexpectedly from the region of the east invaders of obscure race marched in confidence of victory against our land. By main force they easily seized it without striking a blow; and having overpowered the rulers of the land, they then burned our cities ruthlessly, razed to the ground the temples of the gods, and treated all the natives with a cruel hostility, massacring some and leading into slavery the wives and children of others. Finally, they appointed as king one of their number whose name was Salitis. He had his seat at Memphis, levying tribute from Upper and Lower Egypt, and always leaving garrisons behind in the most advantageous places . . . In the Sethroite nome (the part of Egypt to the east of the Nile delta that was named after the god Seth) he found a city very favourably situated on the east of the Bubestite branch of the Nile,[1] and called Avaris after an ancient religious tradition. This place he rebuilt and fortified with massive walls . . .' According to Josephus, the five kings who succeeded Salitis—Bnon, Apachmen, Apophis, Iannas, and Assis

---

[1] In biblical times the Nile had eight branches: today there are only two.

—proved ever 'more and more eager to extirpate the Egyptian stock. Their race as a whole was called "king-shepherds"; for *hyk* in the sacred language means "king" and *sos* in common speech is "shepherd" . . .' Josephus then goes on to adapt in his own words Manetho's account of the subsequent Egyptian revolt against the 'king-shepherds' under the princes of Thebes, who later established the Eighteenth Dynasty: 'Then the kings of Thebes and the rest of Egypt rose in revolt against the shepherds and a great war broke out, which was of long duration. Under a king named Misphrag-mouthosis, the shepherds, he (Manetho) says, were defeated, driven out of all the rest of Egypt and confined in . . . Avaris, containing ten thousand arourae (a measure of land). The shepherds, according to Manetho, enclosed the whole of this area with a great strong wall in order to secure all their possessions and spoils. Thoumosis, the son of Misphrag-mouthosis, invested the walls with an army of four hundred and eighty thousand men and endeavoured to reduce them to submission by siege. Despairing of achieving his object, he concluded a treaty, under which they were all to evacuate Egypt and go whither they would, unmolested. Upon these terms no fewer than two hundred and forty thousand entire households, with their possessions, left Egypt and traversed the desert to Syria . . . they built a city in the country now called Judea, capable of accommodating their vast company, and gave it the name Jerusalem . . .'

After giving a complete history from Egyptian sacred books of the thirty-one Royal dynasties that ruled Egypt from the time of Menes (around 3100 BC) to Alexander the Great (332 BC), Manetho, according to Josephus, provided a separate account, this time from Egyptian folkloric tales, about Moses and the Exodus. Manetho's version describes the Jews led out of Egypt by Osarseph (in Egyptian *wsr-Seph*)[1] as being 'mixed up with a crowd of Egyptian lepers and others, who for various maladies were condemned to banishment from the country'. Although Manetho was clearly describing two separate events—the expulsion of the usurping Hyksos kings by the founders of the Eighteenth Dynasty on the one hand, and the Exodus on the other—Josephus, with understandable anxiety to prove that his ancestors included neither Egyptians nor lepers, identified the Hyksos Asiatic shepherds as being one and the same as the Israelites. He also

[1] This was a case of mistaken identity (see Chapter 12).

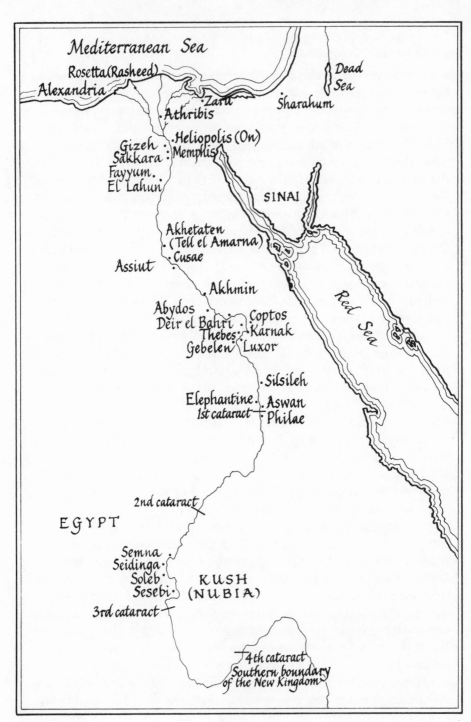

Egypt

attempted to provide etymological support for his view by means of a second definition, again taken from Manetho, of the derivation of the word 'Hyksos', according to which it means 'captive-shepherds', inspired by the Egyptian word for captive, *hyk*.

Nobody today takes seriously Josephus's identification of the Hyksos and the Israelites as the same people. Even Manetho had contradicted Josephus's theory by placing the Exodus—wrongly—during the reign of an Egyptian king named Amenphis (Amenhotep), the eighth ruler in Manetho's king-list of the Eighteenth Dynasty, which is a long time after the Hyksos expulsion. Without making an exhaustive analysis of the matter at this stage, it is worth pointing out again that, while the Hyksos included some Semitic elements, they also had Amurrites and other races among them, and that the Israelites who made the descent to Egypt arrived as peaceful migrants, numbering fewer than seventy persons, not as an invading army.

For the time being the last word on the subject can best be left to Alan Gardiner, the greatest British philologist, who, commenting in his book *Egypt of the Pharaohs* on Josephus's etymology, explained: 'This etymology he prefers because he believed, as do many Egyptologists, that the biblical story of the Israelites' sojourn in Egypt and the subsequent Exodus had as its source the Hyksos occupation and later expulsion. In point of fact, although there are sound linguistic grounds for both etymologies, neither is the true one. The word Hyksos undoubtedly derives from the expression *hik-khase*, "chieftain of a foreign hill country", which from the Middle Kingdom onwards was used to designate Bedouin sheiks. Scarabs bearing this title, but with the word for "countries" in the plural, are found with several un-doubted Hyksos kings . . . It is important to observe, however, that the term refers to the rulers alone, and not, as Josephus thought, to the entire race. Modern scholars have often erred in this matter, some even implying that the Hyksos were a particular race of invaders, who after conquering Syria and Palestine ultimately forced their way into Egypt. Nothing justifies such a view, even though the actual words of Manetho might seem to support it.'

Although modern scholars no longer agree with Josephus on the complete identification of the Israelities with the Hyksos, generally accepting the reign of Ramses II about three centuries later as the right time for the Exodus, the early part of the Hyksos period has retained its ethnic appeal as the era when Joseph was sold into slavery and all his family later followed him down to Egypt. As Eric Peet put it in *Egypt and the Old Testament*: 'Such is the period in which the entry of the Hebrews into Egypt would seem most naturally to fall. It would explain very simply the fact that the newcomers at first met with good treatment at the hands of the "King of Egypt", for from the point of view of a people dwelling in Goshen, probably a region in the eastern delta, the King of Egypt would be the Hyksos reigning at Avaris, doubtless related by race to the Hebrews themselves, and not the Egyptian king reigning, probably in a half-dependent state, at Thebes in Upper Egypt. Should we care to go into details, it would further explain the favour with which Joseph was received by the king, and, should we care to assume that the Jacob tribes were not the first Asiatics to move into the delta, the apportioning to them of the land of Goshen would be merely an incident in the allotment of the captured Egyptian delta to the invading tribes as they arrived.'

However, the fact is that, on studying the biblical narrative carefully and marrying it to Egyptian history, we find that not only does it *not* indicate the Hyksos period as the right time for the Descent of the Israelites into Egypt, it makes such an interpretation impossible.

Chapter 8

CHARIOTS OF WAR ... OR PEACE?

Chariots have played an important part in the debate about when exactly Joseph lived in Egypt. They are mentioned three times in the biblical narration. The first is when Pharaoh appointed Joseph as his vizier:

> And he made him ride in the second chariot which he had; and they cried before him, Bow the knee: and he made him ruler over all the land of Egypt. *Genesis* 41:43.

Again when Jacob arrived in Goshen with his family:

> And Joseph made ready his chariot and went up to meet Israel his father, to Goshen. *Genesis* 46:29.

And for a third time when Joseph went up to Canaan to bury his father:

> And Joseph went up to bury his father: and with him went up all the servants of Pharaoh, the elders of his house, and all the elders of the land of Egypt. And all the house of Joseph, and his brethren, and his father's house: only their little ones, and their flocks, and their herds, they left in the land of Goshen. And there went up with him both chariots and horsemen ... *Genesis* 50:7–9.

It is clear from these verses that chariots were common in Egypt at the time of Joseph, and there is no need to doubt the biblical narration. However, the first of the above references, with Joseph appointed as second-in-command, suggests a responsibility for the chariotry, and considerable scholastic effort has consequently been expended over the years to equip the Hyksos armed forces with chariots of war. For example, William Albright, one writer who frequently associated the Descent into Egypt with the Hyksos conquest, said in his book *The Archaeology of Palestine*: 'The movements of the early seventeenth century BC are still exceedingly obscure, but it seems increasingly probable that a great southward migration of Indo-Aryans and Horites (Hurrians) took place then. There is no trace of these elements in Palestine and southern Syria during the nineteenth century, yet by the fifteenth century Indo-Aryan and Horite princes and nobles were established almost everywhere. Some sort of mass migration of these peoples southward must have occurred meanwhile. By this time horse-drawn chariotry had been introduced as the most important instrument of warfare, and we must picture the northern hordes as sweeping through Palestine and Egypt in swift chariots, with footmen playing a strictly subordinate role.'

We have been asked to accept that a Semite Hyksos ruler would be more likely to appoint a Hebrew like Joseph as his vizier: now, in order to prove the chariot connection, we are asked to accept that the main element among the Hyksos were not, after all, Semites but Indo-Aryan warriors. There is no archaeological evidence whatever to support the view that the Hyksos used chariots to invade Egypt. Nor do they play any significant part in the later struggle to free the country of the usurpers: indeed, in accounts of that struggle it is difficult to find any mention of chariots at all, let alone chariots of war. In 1908, Lord Carnarvon found a tablet in Thebes with hieratic inscriptions giving an account of the early stages of the conflict. It goes as follows: 'In Year 3 of the mighty king in Thebes, Kamose, whom Re had appointed as the real king and granted him power in very sooth, His Majesty spoke in his palace to the council of grandees who were in his suite: "I should like to know what serves this strength of mine when a chieftain is in Avaris, and another in Kush (Nubia), and I sit united with an Asiatic and a Nubian, each man in possession of his slice of this Egypt, and I cannot pass by him as far as Memphis. See, he holds Khmun (modern Ashmun in Middle Egypt), and no man has respite from spoliation through servitude with the Asiatics. I will grapple with him and slit open his belly. My desire is to deliver Egypt and smite the Asiatics."

'Then spoke the grandees of his council: "See, all are loyal to the Asiatics as far as Cusae (a town in Upper Egypt, twenty-five miles north of Asyut). We are tranquil in our part of Egypt. Elephantine is strong, and the middle part is with us as far as Cusae. Men till for us the finest of our lands. Our cattle pasture in the papyrus marshes. Corn is sent for our swine. Our cattle are not taken away."'

However, the king did not agree with his courtiers' advice and decided to go to war to regain the whole of Egypt: 'I fared downstream in might to overthrow the Asiatics by the command of Amun, the just of counsels; my brave army in front of me like a breath of fire, troops of Meda-Nubians aloft upon our cabins to spy out the Asiatics and destroy their places. East and West were in possession of their fat and the army was supplied with things everywhere.'

At this point the text goes on to describe a battle against a Hyksos leader named Teti, the son of Pepi, who had shut himself up within Nefrusi, a city a few miles north of Ashmun: 'I spent the night on my ship, my heart being happy. When the earth came light, I was upon him as it were a hawk. The time of perfuming the mouth (having a meal) came, and I overthrew him, I destroyed his wall, I slew his people and I caused his wife to go down to the river-bank. My soldiers were like lions with their spoils, with slaves, cattle, milk, fat and honey, dividing up their possessions, their hearts being glad. The district of Nefrusi was falling; it was no great thing for us to confine its soul. The region of Per-Shak was lacking when I reached it; their horses were fled within. The garrison . . .'[1]

Here the text comes to an abrupt end. So far, however, there has been no mention of either side using chariots in the fighting, nor that chariots were included among the spoils of battle: the only equine reference is to 'horses fled within'. The narration is resumed in the Kamose Stele[2] which, according to Habachi, is the continuation of the story of the struggle of Kamose against Apophis. The text begins with a phrase that is clearly the latter part of a sentence: '. . . the miserable communication out of your town, while you are forced away together with your army.' It then goes on to describe the fighting that now takes place near Avaris: 'I disposed the fleet of ships furnished with war implements, one ship after the other. I placed prow to stern in my forces, flying over the river as it were a falcon, my warship of gold at the front thereof. . . I caused the strong ship to search the frontier. The navigation after him as it were like a kite uprooting the muddy district of Avaris. I saw his women on the roof of his houses while looking out of their windows . . .'

The stele continues with a series of threats that Kamose intends to

[1] 'A New Rendering of Egyptian Texts', Alan Gardiner in *The Journal of Egyptian Archaeology*, 1918.

[2] This stele was used as a part of the foundation of a statue erected by Ramses II. *Annales du Service*, Issue 53, 1956, Labib Habachi.

put into effect once Avaris is taken and Apophis has been captured: 'I shall drink of the wine of your vineyard, which the Asiatics I captured press out for me; I shall lay waste your dwelling; I shall cut down your trees; I shall drag your women to the ships' holds and I shall seize your chariotry.'

This is the first mention of chariotry in Egyptian records and the only one up to the time of Kamose's brother, Ahmosis I (1575–1550 BC), a century after the appearance of the Hyksos rulers; the fact that it comes at the very end of the king's list, after he had threatened to capture the enemy's women, suggests that the chariots had no military significance but were probably primitive horse-drawn vehicles used simply for transportation.

Kamose, having described the punishment he intended to inflict on the enemy once the war was over, proceeds to give an account of his treatment of those among his countrymen who were helping the enemy: 'I razed their towns and burned their places, they being made into red ruins for ever on account of the damage which they did within this Egypt, and they had made themselves serve the Asiatics and forsaken Egypt their mistress.'

With Apophis safe behind the strong walls of Avaris, out of Kamose's reach, the Theban king left the delta and went back to crush the rebels who still remained behind his extended lines: 'I sent my strong troops which travelled on foot to lay waste Baharia Oasis, while I was in Sako (El-Keis, north of modern Menya), to prevent the rebels being behind me. I went upstream, strong of heart and joyful. I destroyed all the rebels on the road.' After these military achievements, Kamose returned to Thebes where he was received with joy and festivities, only to die shortly afterwards. It is not known what caused his sudden death: his mummy was in such extremely poor condition when it was found that it crumbled to dust in the excavator's hands.

Kamose was succeeded by his brother Ahmosis I, who finally overwhelmed the Hyksos, established the Eighteenth Dynasty and founded the New Kingdom. One of the king's naval officers was Ahmose, the son of Abana, who accompanied the king in his campaigns and later inscribed his autobiography on the walls of his tomb in his native city, El-Kab. This is his account of the eventual fall of Avaris: '. . . I speak to you, all men, I cause you to know the favours that have occurred to me: how I have been rewarded with gold seven times in the sight of the entire land, and with men slaves and women slaves in like manner, and how I have been vested with very many lands. For the name of a valiant man is that which he has done; it will not be obscured in this land for ever . . .

'. . . I had my upbringing in the town of El-Kab, my father being a soldier of the King of Upper and Lower Egypt, the justified Sekenen-re (Kamose's predecessor), whose name was Baba, son of Raonet. I took service as a soldier in his stead, in the ship of *The Wild Bull*, in the time of the Lord of the Two Lands, the justified Nebpehti-re (Ahmosis I), when I was a youth and had not taken a wife, but spent my nights in a hammock of net. Now, when I had established a house,[1] I was taken upon the ship *Northern* because I was valiant; and I used to accompany the Sovereign, on foot, in the course of his going abroad in his chariot. When the town of Avaris was besieged, I showed valour, on foot, in His Majesty's presence. Hereupon I was promoted to the *Manifestation in Memphis*. When they proceeded to fight on the water, in the canal Pa-Dedku of Avaris, I made a capture and brought away a hand,[2] and it was reported to the King's Informant, and the gold of valour was given to me.

'Fighting was repeated in this place, and I proceeded to make a second capture and brought away a hand. And the gold of valour was given to me again. And when they fought in the part of Egypt, south of this town (Avaris), I brought away a male living prisoner. I went down into the water, for he was taken prisoner on the city side, and carried him over the water with me. It was reported to the King's Informant, and thereupon, behold, I was rewarded with gold afresh.

'Then they proceeded to spoil Avaris and I brought away spoil thence: one man, three women, a total of four heads. His Majesty gave them to me for slaves. And they sat down before Sharahum (in south Palestine) for three years. And when His Majesty spoiled it I brought away spoil thence: two women and a hand. And, lo, my spoil was given to me for slaves.'

After the fall of Sharahum, Ahmosis I returned from Palestine, and his next campaign was in the south, in Nubia, before he died after a rule of twenty-two years. His son Amenhotep I followed him and our

[1] The usual phrase for marrying, which indicates that some years must have passed, with Ahmosis I on the throne, between two stages of the campaign against the Hyksos.

[2] It was an Egyptian custom to cut off the hand of a dead enemy as proof of the killing.

son of Abana continued to do battle in the service of the new king. During his twenty-one years on the throne, Amenhotep I fought only in the south; he never followed the Hyksos to the north. Then came his son, Tuthmosis I, and Ahmose, who must have been around sixty by this time, still played a warrior role, having been appointed a captain in the navy. He resumed his autobiography with an account of the wars fought by Tuthmosis I in Syria-Palestine: 'His Majesty arrived at Naharin (Mesopotamia) (and) found that wretch while he was marshalling his forces. His Majesty made a great slaughter among them. There was no counting of the living prisoners which His Majesty brought away from his victories. Now, I was in the front of our army, and His Majesty saw how valiant I was. I brought away a chariot, its horse and him who was in it as living prisoner. These were presented to His Majesty, and I was rewarded with gold another time.'

Ahmose ends his autobiography thus: 'I am grown infirm, I have reached old age, and the favours shown me are like the first . . . I rest in the upland tomb which I myself made.'

From the above accounts of the wars against the Hyksos, first expelling them from Egypt and then following them into Syria-Palestine, we can see that:

1   At the time of Kamose the Egyptians used only naval and foot forces. The Asiatics are said to have horses in their garrison and Kamose promised to capture their chariotry. There is no mention, however, of this chariotry having taken part in any fighting, and Kamose himself refers to having sent his 'strong troops . . . on foot' when he set about the task of quelling the remaining rebels behind his lines.

2   At the time of Ahmosis all we learn on the subject is that the Egyptian king used a chariot in his travels abroad while his valiant officer, Ahmose, accompanied him on foot, which hardly seems likely if chariots had been used in large numbers as military vehicles.

3   At the time of Tuthmosis I, about a quarter of a century after the fall of Avaris and the expulsion of the Hyksos from Egypt, we are given details of a chariot captured in the fighting in Mesopotamia.

There is nothing in this evidence to support the view that the Hyksos used swift chariots in their conflicts with the Egyptians, either at the time of their invasion of the country or their expulsion. It would appear that another quarter of a century elapsed before chariots became an instrument of warfare as opposed to one of simple transport. This is a completely different picture from that given by the Joseph narration in the Pentateuch where, as we saw earlier, Pharaoh made Joseph 'ride in a chariot as his second-in-command' and 'chariots and horsemen' accompanied Joseph when he set out on the journey to Canaan to bury his father.

The fact of the matter is that the whole question of the use of chariots has entered the debate as an assumption on the part of some scholars because they found the Egyptian kings of the Eighteenth Dynasty using chariots. Where did they come from? They concluded that the chariot must have been introduced at the time of the Hyksos invasion.

There have, of course, also been scholars who have taken issue with Albright. Alan Gardiner, one of many who disagree with him, dismissed the notion of 'northern hordes sweeping through Palestine and Egypt'. In his book *Egypt of the Pharaohs* he says: 'It is true that for some centuries past there had been a growing pressure of alien peoples downwards into Syria, Hurrians from the Caspian region being among the first, these paving the way for the Hittites, who followed from the north-west at the end of the sixteenth century. But of such movements there can have been no more than distant repercussions on the Egyptian border. The invasion of the delta by a specific new race is out of the question: one must think rather of an infiltration by Palestinians glad to find refuge in a more peaceful and fertile environment. Some, if not most, of these Palestines were Semites.'

Another aspect of the question is dealt with by John van Seters in his book *The Hyksos*, a doctoral dissertation for Yale University, in which he makes the point: 'One argument in support of a Hurrian element among the Hyksos has to do with the introduction of the horse and chariots into Egypt. This is part of a much wider and more complex problem, the development of chariot warfare. Strong philological evidence indicates that the Mitannians had some competence in the use of the light chariot in warfare and in the training of horses to pull them. This skill, however, must be associated with the Indo-Aryan warrior class, the *maryannu*, and not with the early Hurrians. There is no indication that the Hurrians of the Old Babylonian period (1900–1750 BC) had any advanced ability in this respect. In fact, horsemanship in the Alalakh VII texts'— archaeological digging in Syria-Palestine that indicates Amurrite rule in Syria and Mesopotamia between 1900 and 1700 BC—'is associated entirely with the Amurrites.'

He goes on to conclude, after further discussion of the background: 'The development of Egyptian chariotry probably resulted from the necessity of war in Asia, and not before then. The horse was probably known in Egypt since the time of the Middle Kingdom.[1] Consequently, the use of the horse and chariot in the Hyksos period in Egypt may have been no different from the use of the horse and chariot in the Old Babylonian period in Syria-Palestine. It is hardly possible to postulate an Indo-Aryan, or *maryannu*, element among the Hyksos. This group is unknown in Northern Syria as late as Alalakh VII. The question of chariots, therefore, ought to be dropped from discussion of the Hyksos origins.'

The situation described in the Joseph story could not be found during the time of the Hyksos rulers or in the early period of the Eighteenth Dynasty, as Alan Richard Schulman, the American philologist, has made clear in his valuable research: 'With the apparent exception of a passage in the Stele of Kamose, where the king threatens the Hyksos ruler Apophis, telling him he "will capture the chariotry (*nḥm. it3 nt-ḥtry*)", the Eighteenth Dynasty texts testify to the presence of chariotry as a separate military arm only in the protocols of a few individuals. In all other documents of the period known to me, especially those dealing with the Megiddo campaign of Tuthmosis III, no differentiation was made between the infantry and the chariotry. Although it is true that a distinction was made between "horses" and "foot", one may only read into this that the bulk of the soldiers fought on foot, with the remainder employing chariots. All were equally part of the army (*p3 mš*). If the concept of a special chariotry arm was inherent in the usage of *nt-ḥtry* in the Kamose text, we should certainly expect to find it in the annals of Tuthmosis III as well, but we do not. Consequently, it is reasonable to assume that the term had not yet developed the technical connotation of "chariotry", as distinct from "infantry", which it has in the Ramesside period.

'However, in the later Eighteenth Dynasty two ranks are attested which indicate that such a technical nuance has come into being: Adjutant of the Chariotry (*idnw n t3 nt-ḥtry*), the earliest occurrence of which is known from the Amarna period (of Yuya, who was

---

[1] The skeleton of a horse was found at Buhen in a Middle Kingdom context.

appointed as Adjutant (Deputy) of His Majesty in the Chariotry as well as Officer for the Horses), and The Standard-Bearer of the Chariot-Warrior . . . which is recorded on the stele of Meryptah and which dates, most probably, to the early years of the reign of Amenhotep III. It would thus seem that by this reign (Amenhotep III) chariotry was thought of as a separate entity, and we may assume that the army had been reorganised into the two arms of infantry and chariotry, each with its own organic and administrative components, at about that time.'[1]

Thus the first person in Egypt to be appointed to the position ascribed to Joseph in the Bible was Yuya, the vizier of Amenhotep III. This, however, is far from being the only evidence that points to Joseph and Yuya being one and the same person.

[1] *Journal of the American Research Centre in Egypt*, Issue 2, 1963.

Chapter 9

THE EGYPT OF JOSEPH

The other indications that Joseph lived in Egypt during the Eighteenth Dynasty, rather than more than two centuries earlier during the Hyksos period, are inevitably fragmentary, but so compelling that it seems remarkable that nobody has gathered them all together before and drawn from them the obvious conclusion. To place them in the same chronology as the story of Joseph in the Pentateuch and the Koran . . .

SLAVERY IN ANCIENT EGYPT

And Joseph was brought down to Egypt; and Potiphar, an officer of Pharaoh, captain of the guard, an Egyptian, bought him of the hands of the Ishmaelites, which had brought him down thither. *Genesis* 39:1.

When might such a slave transaction have taken place in ancient Egypt? As Donald B. Redford pointed out in his book *A Study of the Biblical Story of Joseph*, Asiatics had probably been present in Egypt from the beginning of her history. Punitive raids by the Egyptian army had been responsible for some, while others must have arrived by other means, perhaps as free aliens who, as guests, had been permitted to enter Egypt along with goods from Syria procured through trade. Under Amenemhet III, and during the Thirteenth Dynasty, a fairly sizeable foreign element can be detected in the population of Egypt. The Asiatics who appear in the roster of workers at the Sinai mines seem to be there because of their specialised skills. There are donkey drivers, soldiers and even chieftains from Palestine. This bespeaks co-operation between Egyptians and Asiatics, not enslavement of the latter by the former.

Around the middle of the sixteenth century BC, with the beginning of the Eighteenth Dynasty after the Hyksos expulsion, slaves of

Palestinian or Syrian origin began to appear in Egypt in large numbers. This influx was the result of military conquest in Asia where Tuthmosis III's campaigns alone are said to have brought seven thousand captives. These prisoners were regarded as Royal property, and it was the king, as we saw in the case of Ahmose, who could give them to his officers or assign them to the temple. There is also evidence that slaves were bought and sold for silver or property during the Eighteenth Dynasty. Abd el-Mohsen Bakir, the Egyptian scholar, in his research concerning slavery in the different periods of ancient Egypt, was able to find some legal documents, referring to transactions involving slaves and starting from the Eighteenth Dynasty. He concluded his account in *Slavery in Pharaonic Egypt* by saying: 'From the evidence before us, slavery, strictly speaking, existed between the Eighteenth and Twenty-second Dynasties, while before and after that period only various degrees of "bondage" can be demonstrated.'

It therefore follows that, if the story of Joseph in the Pentateuch is giving a factual report of his being sold into Egypt as a slave, by merchants for silver, this account could not possibly be accurate unless the transaction took place at some time between the Eighteenth and Twenty-second Dynasties.

POTIPHAR

I suspect this to have been a title rather than an actual name. It is almost identical with Potipherah, the priest of On, whose daughter was given to Joseph by Pharaoh as a wife. There is a pattern into which the references to both names fall. In the case of Joseph, cited above, we are told that 'Potiphar, an officer of Pharaoh, captain of the guard, an Egyptian, bought him . . .' Similarly, the two mentions of Joseph's wife read:

And Pharaoh . . . gave him to wife Asenath, the daughter of Potipherah, priest of On. *Genesis* 41:45.

And unto Joseph were born two sons before the year of famine came, which Asenath, the daughter of Potipherah, the priest of On, bare unto him. *Genesis* 41:50.

In each case it is possible to divide the name into three elements: Pharaoh (phar, pherah) Poti, and a position (captain of the guard, the priest of On). Although the matter still needs further research, I feel the names might be interpreted as 'captain of the guard, the appointed one of Pharaoh and 'the priest of On, the appointed one of Pharaoh'.

We find a similar reference in the next book of the Pentateuch:

> And Eleazar, Aaron's son, took him one of the daughters of Puti-el (Poti-el) to wife . . . *Exodus* 6:25.

This verse indicates the composite nature of the name and, if the same approach is taken, this reference can be interpreted as: 'Puti, the given one of God'.

At the same time, if Potiphar is to be taken as an actual name, scholars have pointed out that it is also the Egyptian *p3-di-p3-R'* (He whom Re gives), of which three examples have been found in Egyptian texts. One is found on a stele in Cairo which can be dated no earlier than the Twenty-first Dynasty. The other two are in demotic, the late, simplified Egyptian form of writing, one from the Twenty-first Dynasty and the other from the third century BC. If Potiphar is an actual name the comments of Donald B. Redford in his book *A Study of the Biblical Story of Joseph* are relevant. He points out that, because of the presence of the definite article, *p3*, names of this type are not likely to be found before the introduction of Late Egyptian as fashionable literary dialect during the reign of Akhnaten, Yuya's grandson, in the last third of the Eighteenth Dynasty.

JOSEPH'S PRISON

The prison where Joseph was kept has a special name, *bet-hassohar*, which is repeated six times in Genesis. Neither the origin nor meaning of the word *sohar* is clear. Dictionaries, including *A Hebrew and English Lexicon of the Old Testament*, published in 1907, relate it to the word *sahar*, which means 'to be round', and they consider this house (*bet*) or construction to be part of a fortification system. The result of this interpretation is that Joseph, together with the king's prisoners, was condemned to detention and forced to work in a fortress. As the name *bet-hassohar* for prison occurs only in the Joseph narration, and is applied exclusively to an Egyptian prison, it is thought probable that the word itself could be Egyptian. This accords perfectly with the Egyptian inscriptions of the Eighteenth Dynasty and also the Decree of Horemheb,[1] the last of its kings, who ordered that people guilty of having hindered the delivery of certain taxes should have their noses cut off and be sent to the fortress *ṯ3rw* (Zaru).

A. S. Yahuda, who was convinced that it was an Egyptian word, developed this theme in his book *The Language of the Pentateuch in its Relation to Egyptian*, in which, after a discussion of the semantics involved,[2] he says: 'As to *ṯ3r* itself, it occurs more in inscriptions of the New Kingdom than of any other time as the name of a fortress close to the Palestine frontier to which corrupt officials and notorious criminals were consigned. It appears for the first time in an inscription of Tuthmosis III about 1478 BC, reporting a campaign undertaken by him from this spot in the twenty-second year of his reign "to enlarge the borders of Egypt".'

Yahuda goes on to explain: 'All this shows that everywhere *ṯ3r* is spoken of as a very well-known fortress of great strategic and military importance. This and the use of the fortress as a penal establishment make it highly probable that it is identical with *sohar*, so that the narrator of the Joseph story actually meant this fortress. From the Edict of Horemheb we see furthermore that *ṯ3r* is simply mentioned as a place for the internment of criminals, exactly in the same laconic way as in the Joseph story . . .'

Although Joseph Vergote was able to show that Yahuda's reading of *sohar* and *ṯ3r* was not possible on philological grounds, he still thought it possible that *ṯ3r* was the prison where Joseph was kept. As Yahuda considers that the events of the Joseph story took place even before the Hyksos period in Egypt, he tried to show that the fortress, which was mentioned for the first time in the inscription of Tuthmosis III in Karnak relating to his wars in Syria, had already existed from the

---

[1] In the aftermath of the religious revolution inspired by Amenhotep IV (Akhnaten), Horemheb, who succeeded the Amarna kings, issued a number of punitive Decrees or Edicts designed to restore stability to the country.

[2] 'In many Egyptian inscriptions we find the word *ṯ3r*, which is also transcribed *ṯ3 rw* with a final vowel. From a phonetic point of view, *ṯ3r* fully corresponds to *sohar*, as Egyptian *ṯ* is quite regularly equivalent to Hebrew *s* (*samekh*), and Egyptian *3* (*aleph*) is frequently represented in Hebrew by *h* (*he*) so that the transcription of *ṯ3r* by *shr* would be perfectly correct.'

This no doubt seems somewhat puzzling, but different languages have different letters for the same sound. In English, for instance, we have 'B' and 'V', but the Spaniards normally pronounce both as 'B'.

time of the Twelfth Dynasty. It is true that at the same place there was an ancient fortress mentioned in the autobiography of Sinuhe, dating from the Twelfth Dynasty, but then it had a different name—the Pathes of Horus.

Once Joseph finds himself in Pharaoh's good offices after interpreting his dreams, is released from prison and appointed vizier, we find ourselves with several incidents that, yet again, point to the Eighteenth Dynasty as the time that he lived and became an influential figure in Egyptian life.

THE TWO LANDS

And Pharaoh said unto Joseph, See, I have set thee over all the land of Egypt. *Genesis* 41:41.

The Hebrew word for Egypt, *miṣrim*, is in the plural and means literally 'the two Egypts'. This is explained simply by the fact that it is an adaptation of the Egyptian *t3wy* (the Two Lands). Lord of the Two Lands was the official title of Pharaoh. So the Hebrew bible, which refers to Joseph being appointed by Pharaoh as having jurisdiction over 'the whole country of the Two Lands' rather than simply 'the whole country', emphasises that both Upper and Lower Egypt were placed under Joseph's control.

Yahuda observed in his book *The Language of the Pentateuch in its Relation to Egyptian*: 'It is noteworthy that in the Joseph narrative, especially when Joseph's official activities are referred to, the formal expression *b-kul ard miṣrim* (over all the country of the Two Lands) is frequent, whereas elsewhere it reads merely *b-ard miṣrim* (over the country of the Two Lands). The question arises whether this seemingly casual use of the two phrases was not as a matter of fact intentional. In order to appreciate the far-reaching importance of this question in its right light, it is necessary first of all to make some observations on the origin and meaning of *miṣrim* as a name for Egypt, especially as this of itself is of no little interest.

'The striking feature of this name is its dual form. It has been variously assumed that the dual form is to be explained by the division of the country into Upper and Lower Egypt. This is doubtless quite right: nevertheless there is no unanimity as to the meaning of the word *msr*, from which the dual is formed. While some explain it by the

Aramaic *miṣra* (Akkadian *miṣru*, "boundary") others connect it with the Hebrew *mṣur*, interpreted as equivalent to "fortress'. But on closer examination it becomes obvious that *miṣrim* is nothing else than a literal and grammatical adaptation of the Egyptian word *t3wy*, dual of *t3* (land)—that is the Two Lands or the "twin lands", this being as a matter of fact the designation given by the Egyptians to their country from time immemorial with reference to Upper and Lower Egypt.'

Yet as we saw from the evidence of the Carnarvon Tablet and the Kamose Stele, Egypt, during the Hyksos period, was divided into three different parts: Lower and Middle Egypt were under control of the Hyksos while Upper Egypt was still under Egyptian rule and Nubia was under a native ruler. There were definite boundaries between them: Cusae between the Hyksos and Upper Egypt, Elephantine between Upper Egypt and Nubia. As Gardiner has concluded (in *Egypt of the Pharaohs*): 'The whole tenor of the great inscription makes it clear that Apophis, presumably the last of his name, never extended his rule beyond Khmun, except for a quite temporary occupation of Gebelen (Pi-Ḥatḥor); and there is no real evidence that any other member of his race had ever done so either.'

The Hyksos rulers never, at any stage of their rule, controlled *miṣrim*, the Two Lands of Egypt. In this case, if Joseph was appointed to his position under a Hyksos ruler, the Biblical statement referring to 'the whole of the country of the Two Lands', which the biblical narrator seems to have been at pains to stress in certain circumstances, would not have been possible.

ABREK

And he (Pharaoh) made him ride in the second chariot which he had; and they cried before him, Bow the knee . . . *Genesis* 41:43

The expression 'Bow the knee' is an English translation of the Hebrew word *abrek*, which according to Joseph Vergote (*Joseph en Egypte*) derives from an Egyptian imperative meaning 'do obeisance' and is known[1] to have entered Egyptian as a loan word during the New Kingdom as a command by the herald to spectators to prostrate themselves. It did not exist in Egyptian vocabulary before the time of the Eighteenth Dynasty.

---

[1] *A Study of the Biblical Story of Joseph*, Donald B. Redford. Also *Egyptian Loan Words and Transcriptions*, T. O. Lambdin.

JOSEPH'S NAME
And Pharaoh called Joseph's name Zaphnath-pa-a-neah; and he gave him to wife Asenath, the daughter of Potipherah, priest of On . . . *Genesis* 41:45.

It is natural that Pharaoh should have given Joseph an Egyptian name on his elevation to the position of vizier. To Egyptians one's name had a separate entity and was part of the spiritual being of a person. By giving Joseph a new name, Pharaoh was at the same time giving him a new Egyptian identity. The origin of the name—*s ph ntr iw-f 'nh* (*Seph-net-pana neh*) in Egyptian—has been the source of discussion and argument for nearly a century, with Hebrew scholars seeking an interpretation that would reflect Joseph's role in the Bible (see Book Two, Chapter 4).

The main elements of the name are *s ph* (time), *ntr* (god) with the conventional *iw-f 'nh* (may he live), which would mean: 'Time of god, may he live'. Although he is always referred to as Joseph in the Bible, there is no means of knowing precisely the name by which the man was known when he first arrived in Egypt from Canaan. It may have been simply one syllable, relating him to his God, *Yhwa* (Jehovah). It was the custom at the time for the full form of the divine name to be used only by the priestly class: others used a diminutive. In his book *The World of the Old Testament*, Cyrus H. Gordon makes the point that the name *Yhwa* 'may be an expansion of a shorter form: cf. Yo, Yeho, Yah and Yahu, which also occur'. In addition, there has been a suggestion that the divine name is on a stone found at Ras Shamra in Syria where Yu figures as the son of the god El (Elohim),[1] and it is also thought that the name of Joseph's father was at one time Y/ and was expanded later, sometimes to Jacob, sometimes to Israel (*Yisra-el*). It seems to me that, in giving Joseph his new name, Pharaoh probably replaced the monosyllable *Yu*, relating Joseph to his God, with the Egyptian word for 'god'. While *el* is usually placed as a suffix in proper nouns, as in Israel, the *Y* of *Yhwa* normally appears as a prefix, as in Jacob.

As the word 'Seph' does not seem to have a Hebrew origin, it is more likely that it derives from Egyptian. *Sp(Sph)* is an Egyptian name meaning 'time' and was used as a name for both men and women

[1] *Les Découvertes des Ras Shamra et l'Ancien Testament*, R. H. R. Dassaud.

during the Old, Middle and New Kingdoms of Egypt where we have these examples: *Sp, Sp-wr.t, Sp-n, Sp-n-wrdt.t, Sp-n.mw-t, Sp-nfr, Sp-y, Sp-s* (*Die Ägyptischen Personennamen*, Hermann Ranke). It therefore seems likely that the Patriarch was not known as 'Joseph' from the time of his birth, but was given this name—adopted ultimately by the biblical narrators—later in his life.

Zaphnath-pa-a-neah does not point to any particular period for Joseph's life in Egypt, but the name of his wife provides another clue.

JOSEPH'S WIFE

Asenath, the biblical name of Joseph's wife, is derived from the Egyptian *ns-nt*, which scholars have chosen to interpret as meaning 'belonging to the goddess Neit'.[1] Although this is the only example we know of that incorporates the goddess Neit, similar names incorporating other gods and goddesses were common in Egypt from the time of the Old Kingdom, and, in view of the evidence found in Tuya's tomb, it is important to bear in mind that, as there are no vowels in hieroglyphics, *ns-nt* can equally well be interpreted as 'belonging to the goddess Nut'. In his book *A Study of the Biblical Story of Joseph*, Donald B. Redford adopted Sethe's interpretation. As the Hebrew transcription of the name has an initial '*a*' instead of the '*n*' to be found in the Egyptian form, this was seen by Redford as representing a later stage in the development of the name. The earliest example known dates, in fact, from the time of the Twenty-sixth Dynasty. However, Joseph Vergote in his book *Joseph en Egypte* refused to follow Sethe in this reading, preferring to adopt an interpretation by W. Spiegelberg of an Egyptian name that corresponds exactly with the biblical transcription Asenath, *iw.s-n-t*. This form, which has substantially the same meaning—she belongs to Neit—derives from the Lower Egyptian dialect and a stage in the development of the Egyptian language, known as neo-Egyptian, that originated during the Eighteenth Dynasty and started to be used in writing from the time of the Amarna kings, Yuya's descendants. No matter which of the above interpretations is followed, the biblical form of the name of Joseph's wife clearly cannot date from the Hyksos era.

Another aspect of Asenath, pointing away from the Hyksos period,

---

[1] *Das Ägyptische Verbum*, K. Sethe.

is the description of her as the 'daughter of the priest of On' (Helio-polis), which was the centre of the Egyptian worship of the sun-god Re. Yet we know that the Hyksos honoured only one Egyptian god, Seth, whom the Egyptians themselves hated, as the murderer of the good Osiris, although they feared and worshipped him as well. Manetho has related how they razed the temples of the other gods to the ground. J. B. Pritchard records in his book *Ancient Near Eastern Texts* that, about a century after the Hyksos expulsion from Egypt, Queen Hatshepsut still remembered their hostility towards Egyptian worship: 'I have restored that which had been ruined. I raised up that which had gone to pieces formerly, since the Asiatics were in the midst of Avaris of the Northland, and vagabonds were in the midst of them, overthrowing that which had been made. They ruled without Re and did not act by divine command.'

The Hyksos attachment to Seth is described in the Papyrus Sallier I (British Museum No. 10185), which was written during the late Nineteenth Dynasty: 'King Apophis made him Seth as Lord, and he would not serve any god who was in the land except Seth. And he built a temple of good and eternal work beside the house of King Apophis, and appeared every day to have sacrifices made . . . to Seth.' This account was confirmed by the discovery of an offering table, dating from the time of Apophis and bearing the inscription 'he made it as a monument for his father, Seth, Lord of Avaris.' In *Egypt of the Pharaohs*, Alan Gardiner connects Seth of Avaris with an Asiatic god: 'At Avaris, the Hyksos worshipped the strange animal-god Seth . . . in the temple reliefs and elsewhere. He has been mentioned already as the enemy and murderer of the good god Osiris, but the Hyksos chose to ignore that regrettable aspect, as indeed had been done in this remote corner of the delta from the earliest times. Their version of Seth, now written in Babylonian fashion as though pronounced Sutekh, was certainly more Asiatic in character than the native original, bearing in his garment and head-dress a distinct resemblance to the Semitic Ba'al . . .' Why, then, would a Hyksos ruler, who himself worshipped Seth, marry his new friend and vizier to a daughter of a priest of the hated (by the Hyksos) god Re? Eric Peet, despite favouring the Hyksos period for Joseph's descent into Egypt, had to confess in his book *Egypt and the Old Testament* that he found this matter of the marriage mystifying and beyond his acceptance: 'If we suppose with most commentators that Joseph was a Semite who rose to favour under a

Hyksos (Semitic) king, and that the oppression only began after the expulsion of the Hyksos, when the Egyptian kings of the Eighteenth Dynasty reconquered the delta, we must admit that the Hyksos king not only allowed the worship of Re to continue at Heliopolis, but even encouraged his favourite Joseph to marry the daughter of Re's priest. All that we know of the Hyksos occupation of Egypt from the Egyptian side makes such an admission very difficult, and it is almost beyond doubt that the story of this marriage, like the names of the priest and his daughter, cannot date from Hyksos times, but is a later colouring.'

THE DREAMER KING

Tuthmosis IV, who I believe appointed Joseph as his vizier, was, like Joseph, a dreamer, as we saw earlier from the account of the Sphinx and the sand, and would therefore be more likely to have an empathy with an interpreter of dreams.[1]

The journeys that Joseph's brothers made down to Egypt to buy corn at the time of famine provide further evidence that these journeys took place during the period of the Eighteenth Dynasty rather than more than two centuries earlier.

---

[1] It is interesting that Jewish rabbinical literature provides another story that fits in exactly with the story to be found on the stele between the forelegs of the Sphinx. In section Mikkez of Sefer ha-Yasher in the Haggadah we are told that, when Joseph interpreted Pharaoh's dream, the king asked for a sign by which he might know that the interpretation was true. Joseph told him that the queen, who was about to be delivered of a child, would give birth to a son who would be the next Pharaoh. The king—Amenhotep II, in my view—was puzzled to hear this as he already had a two-year-old son who, in the normal course of events, would succeed him on the throne. Joseph explained, however, that this elder son would die and it was the younger one who would be the future king. This is exactly what happened, and, on coming to the throne, Tuthmosis, who must have been aware of Joseph's prophecy even before he had his own vision at the Sphinx, appointed Joseph as his vizier.

This sequence of events, in which it was necessary for Joseph to provide a sign, would explain the indication in the Koran that some time elapsed between Joseph's interpretation of Pharaoh's dreams and his actual release from prison because he refused to be discharged until the false charge against him had been withdrawn.

In introducing this story, however, The Jewish Encyclopaedia provides another indication of the uncertain world we enter with biblical characters when it comes to figures. Various sources are quoted giving the length of time Joseph spent in prison as ranging from one to as high as twelve years.

THE ACCUSATION OF SPYING

When his brothers first appeared and Joseph recognised them, he concealed his own identity and spoke to them harshly:

> . . . Ye are spies; to see the nakedness of the land ye are come.
> *Genesis* 42:9.

The way in which the word for spies (*meraggelim*) occurs in the Old Testament makes it clear that it signifies what we might call 'intelligence agents', sent out just prior to a major military campaign. The mere presence of *meraggelim* was considered an indication of an invasion to come. If the brothers had appeared at the time when the rulers were the Hyksos, the majority of whose followers were also Canaanites, they could hardly have been accused of spying.

JOSEPH'S OATH

After the brothers have denied the charge, Joseph demands that his younger brother, Benjamin, be brought down to Egypt, and twice swears an oath in the course of addressing them:

> '. . . Hereby ye shall be proved. By the life of Pharaoh ye shall not go forth hence, except your youngest brother come hither. Send one of you, and let him fetch your brother, and ye shall be kept in prison, that your words may be proved, whether there be any truth in you: or else by the life of Pharaoh surely ye are spies.'
> *Genesis* 42:15,16.

This form of oath did not exist in Egypt before the Eighteenth Dynasty and the New Kingdom. According to Abd el-Mohsen Bakir in his book *Slavery in Pharaonic Egypt*, the oath formula during the Eighteenth Dynasty was initially, 'As Amun endures and the Ruler endures' and changed later into, 'As Amun lives and as Pharaoh lives.'

THE INTERPRETER

On the third day of their imprisonment, Joseph visited the brothers to repeat his demand that the younger brother should be brought down to Egypt, and overheard a conversation between them:

> And Reuben answered them, saying, 'Spake I not unto you, saying, Do not sin against the child (Joseph); and ye would not

hear? therefore, behold, his blood is required. And they knew not that Joseph understood them; for he spake unto them by an interpreter. *Genesis* 42:22, 23.

Canaanite was the language of the Hyksos rulers and, had they been dealing with a Hyksos vizier, the brothers would not have expected him to need the services of an interpreter. Nor would they have conducted in his presence what was clearly meant to be a private conversation if they had had any suspicion that he might understand what they were saying.

THE METHOD OF PAYMENT

In the Joseph narration the brothers use money to pay for the grain they buy in Egypt:

Then Joseph commanded to fill their sacks with corn, and to restore every man's money into his sack, and to give them provision for the way . . . *Genesis* 42:25.

It used to be thought that money came into use in Egypt only from the time of Sheshonq I of the Twenty-second Dynasty (950 BC), and that prior to this period the form of such a transaction as buying grain would be the exchange of goods of equivalent value. The obvious assumption was made that the compilers of Genesis had expressed the customs of their own era when they wrote of payment by silver. However, recent studies have found evidence to support the idea that, at least from the reign of Amenhotep II, pieces of metal—gold, silver and copper, of a fixed weight and value—were used as a means of exchange.[1] Bakir also points out in *Slavery in Pharaonic Egypt* that a reference in a legal document of the Eighteenth Dynasty indicates that 'two debens of silver' were paid as a price for a slave. The role that money played in grain purchase in the biblical story of Joseph therefore again conforms with the situation that existed in Egypt during the New Kingdom.

---

[1] 'Prices and Wages in Egypt in the Ramesside Period', in *Cahiers d'histoire mondial*, No. 4, 1954. Also 'Un Document sur la vie chère à Thèbes au début de la XVIII° dynastie', in the *Bulletin of the Société Française d'Egypte*, No. 12, 1953, E. Drioton.

THE MANY-GATED CITY

According to the Koran, Jacob asked his sons, before their second corn-buying journey to Egypt, accompanied by Joseph's full brother, Benjamin, not to enter the city by one gate:

> Further he said:
> 'O my sons! enter not
> All by one gate: enter ye
> By different gates . . .
> *Sura* XII:67.

This same story is found in Jewish traditions:

> His brothers, fearing the evil eye, entered the city at ten different gates. *Midrash Bereshith Rabbah 89, Tanchumah, Mikkez 3, Sefer Ha-Yasar.*

As this was the brothers' second visit, it is reasonable to assume that Jacob could only have known anything about the city from hearing details of their previous trip. Which city did the brothers visit—Avaris, the Hyksos capital in the eastern delta, or Thebes, the capital of the Eighteenth Dynasty kings on the Upper Nile?

We know from Manetho's account that Avaris was 'fortified with massive walls' and that it was captured eventually by Ahmosis I only after a bitter struggle lasting many years. Avaris, whose very name in ancient Egyptian suggests a castle or fortress, could not have had anything like ten different gates for the brothers to use in entering the city. Thebes, on the other hand, was never walled, although it was always known throughout the ancient world to be 'the city with many gates' and the Greek poet Homer mentioned it about the tenth century BC as 'the hundred-gated city'. This does not refer to entrances through the city's walls, but to gates belonging to its temples and palaces. Jacob's advice to his sons therefore makes sense only if they were returning to Thebes, not Avaris.

AN ABOMINATION OF SHEPHERDS

The biblical narrator refers on two occasions to the Hebrew shepherds as being an abomination to Egyptians. The first occurs when Joseph's brothers return, bringing Benjamin with them, and are invited to a meal at Joseph's home:

Coffer from the tomb of Yuya, providing evidence that he lived and died during the reign of Amenhotep III. The lid of the coffer (*right*) is adorned with the names of Amenhotep and Tiye. *Photos: Cairo Museum*

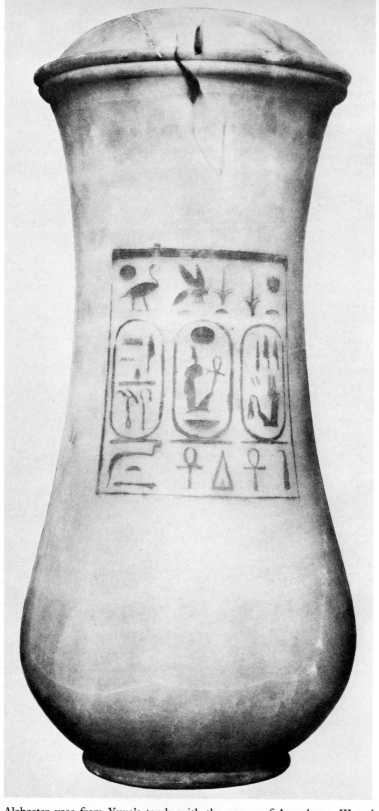

Alabaster vase from Yuya's tomb, with the names of Amenhotep III and
Queen Tiye. *Photo: Cairo Museum*

One of three chairs found in Yuya's tomb, which had previously belonged to the Princess Sitamun at various stages in her childhood. This one, the smallest, measures 595mm high, 400mm wide and 370mm deep. *Photo: Cairo Museum*

Sitamun's second chair, measuring 615mm high, 380mm wide and 410mm deep. *Photo: Cairo Museum*

Back view of the smallest chair. *Photo: Cairo Museum*

Front and side views of the largest chair, measuring 770mm high, 520mm wide and 540mm deep. Both this and the second chair are decorated with scenes showing Sitamun herself and are inscribed with her name. *Photos: Cairo Museum*

Sitamun's kohl-tube of bright blue, glazed faience, probably from her palace at Thebes. It is inscribed with the names of Amenhotep III and Sitamun, who is described as 'daughter of a king' and 'wife of a king'. *Photo:*

Sandstone block with a bas-relief carving of Queen Sitamun. She carries the royal 'flail', and her name, partly broken, appears in a cartouche above her head. The vulture head-dress belongs to a royal heiress, God's wife of Amun, the same as that worn by pre-Amarna queens of the Eighteenth Dynasty. It was found by Petrie in the Temple of Amenhotep II. *Photo: Petrie Museum, University College, London*

The chariot found in Yuya's tomb. Its small size suggests that it was not designed for normal use. Yuya was the first person in Egyptian history to be given the titles 'Master of the Horse' and 'Deputy of His Majesty in the Chariotry', titles which the Bible ascribes to Joseph. *Photos: Cairo Museum*

Ramses II, found at Thebes and removed by Belzoni on behalf of the British Consul-General. *Photo: British Museum*

Colossus of Ramses, excavated by Mariette at Tanis. *Photo: Cairo Museum*

The Israel Stele of Merenptah, discovered by Petrie at Thebes in 1896. *Photo: Cairo Museum*

Detail of the Israel Stele, showing the name of Israel. *Photo: Cairo Museum*

> And they set on for him (Joseph) by himself and for them by themselves, and for the Egyptians, which did eat with him, by themselves: because the Egyptians might not eat bread with the Hebrews; for that is an abomination unto the Egyptians. *Genesis* 43:32.

The second occurs after the tribe of Israel has arrived in Egypt to settle and Joseph's brothers are about to have an audience with Pharaoh. He warns them:

> And it shall come to pass, when Pharaoh shall call you, and shall say, 'What is your occupation?' That ye shall say, Thy servants' trade hath been about cattle from our youth even until now, both we, and also our fathers: that ye may dwell in the land of Goshen; for every shepherd is an abomination unto the Egyptians. *Genesis* 46:33, 34.

It is difficult to imagine that a Hyksos, himself a ruler of shepherds, would consider Joseph's family an abomination on account of their being shepherds. The Egyptian evidence shows that it was during the Eighteenth Dynasty, after the expulsion of the Hyksos, that Asiatic shepherds became particularly disliked.

THE AGRARIAN REFORMS

Chapter 47 of the Book of Genesis is devoted to an account of how, in the course of Joseph's preparations for the impending seven years of famine, all the land of Egypt came into Pharaoh's possession. Various attempts have been made, without success, to relate this to some specific period of Egyptian history. I, personally, share the view of Joseph Vergote, who says in his book *Joseph en Egypte* that he considers the table of the patriarch Joseph's agricultural policy to be an invention on the part of the Hebrew narrator and sees no point in trying to relate it to a particular Pharaonic time. In any case, if Joseph had foreseen the famine and prepared for it one would not expect it to be written about at any length.

Incidentally, Amenhotep III appears in a scene in the tomb of Anen, Yuya's son, sitting inside a granary in a harvest festival celebration.[1]

---

[1] *Topographial Bibliography of Ancient Egyptian Hieroglyphic Texts, Reliefs and Paintings*, Bertha Porter and Rosalind Moss.

THE EMBALMING OF JACOB

After the death of Jacob in Egypt, he was mummified on Joseph's personal instructions:

> And Joseph commanded his servants the physicians to embalm his father: and the physicians embalmed Israel. And forty days were fulfilled for him; for so are fulfilled the days of those who are embalmed: and the Egyptians mourned for him threescore and ten days. *Genesis* 50:2, 3.

From their earliest times, the Egyptians tried to preserve human as well as animal bodies after death. They believed that the spiritual element in a person leaves the body at the time of death, but would one day return provided that the body had not been destroyed. It was because of this belief that, from the early days of the Old Kingdom, they worked at developing the techniques of mummification. As it was an expensive process, only members of the Royal family were able to afford mummification initially. By the time of the New Kingdom, the Eighteenth to Twentieth Dynasties, nobles and officials, too, were receiving this treatment, but ordinary people were not able to have their dead mummified until after the end of the dynastic period.

The Greek historian, Herodotus, who visited Egypt in the fifth century BC, described the mummification process, and his account agrees with the biblical statement that it took seventy days. About half of this time—forty days according to Genesis—was required for dehydration of the body.

Mummification was associated virtually from the beginning with belief in the resurrection of Osiris, a dead god, ruler of the underworld and judge of the dead. Osiris remained the symbol of resurrection until Roman times, when belief in Jesus Christ replaced this ancient Egyptian creed, but even then it was a long time before Egyptian Copts (native Christians of the Jacobite sect of Monophysites) abandoned completely the practice of mummification.

Osiris had been assassinated by his brother Seth (Sutekh), who, as we saw earlier, was the only Egyptian god worshipped by the Hyksos. Why would a follower of Seth observe the Osiris practice of mummification and accept his judgement in the afterworld? In fact, from the archaeological evidence available not a single case is known of a Hyksos ruler, or any of their officials, being mummified; nor has a tomb, in the Egyptian form, ever been found for one of the Hyksos rulers of the country. Scarabs and Tell el-Yahudiyah ware of the Hyksos period were found in a brick-built tomb with corbelled roof at Tell el-Yahudiyah,[1] but this and similar structured tombs, built usually within a city, contained multiple burials and were more probably intended as family vaults.

The biblical mention of the mummification of Jacob and, later, Joseph can be only a memory of a true event in the life and experience of the early Israelites. It cannot be a subsequent insertion because it is completely against the later Jewish beliefs. Furthermore, not only was mummification not practised by the Hyksos: the earliest reference we have to the embalming process lasting seventy days comes from the Eighteenth Dynasty,[2] again suggesting that Jacob and Joseph could not have been mummified during the time of the Hyksos rule.

---

[1] *Hyksos and Israelite Cities*, W. M. Flinders Petrie.

[2] 'The Tombs of Djehuty and Antef', in *Studies in Honour of F. Ll Griffith*, N. de G. Davies; *idem The Tomb of Amenemhet*, Alan Gardiner.

Chapter 10

THE LOST CITIES

In addition to the evidence given in the previous chapter, supporters of the Hyksos-to-Ramses II theory are faced with a paradox over where Joseph's family actually settled. The implication of the story in Genesis is that the Israelites, who were looked upon as 'detestable' because they were shepherds, found themselves banished to a region called Goshen, remote from the palace, where they would not give offence to their Egyptian hosts. Yet when we turn to the Book of Exodus we find them living on Pharaoh's doorstep. After the account of how Moses, at the age of three months, was hidden among the reeds because of Pharaoh's command that all male Hebrew children should be murdered, we read:

> And the daughter of Pharaoh came down to wash herself at the river; and her maidens walked along by the river's side; and when she saw the ark among the flags, she sent her maid to fetch it. And when she had opened it, she saw the child: and, behold, the babe wept. And she had compassion on him, and said, This is one of the Hebrews' children. *Exodus* 2:5, 6.

The same proximity is inherent in the story of enslavement of the Hebrews that takes up much of the early part of the second book of the Pentateuch and results ultimately in the Exodus:

> Now there arose up a new king over Egypt, which knew not Joseph. And he said unto his people, Behold the people of the children of Israel are more and mightier than we: Come on, let us deal wisely with them; lest they multiply, and it come to pass that, when there falleth out any war, they join also unto our enemies, and fight against us, and so get them up out of the land.
>
> Therefore they did set over them taskmasters to afflict them with their burdens. And they built for Pharaoh treasure cities,

Pi-thom and Ra-am-ses. But the more they afflicted them, the more they multiplied and grew. And they were grieved because of the children of Israel. And the Egyptians made the children of Israel to serve with rigour: And they made their lives bitter with hard bondage, in morter, and in brick, and in all manner of service in the field . . . *Exodus* 1:8–14.

The situation is therefore exactly the opposite of what one might expect. The Hyksos, themselves shepherds, are said to have banished the pastoral Canaanites to a distant region, while the rulers of the time of Moses, whom we are led to believe would have found the Israelites anathema, have them living within walking distance.

The Exodus itself, which followed the Oppression and had been foretold by Joseph, is also said to have started from Ramses:

And the children of Israel journeyed from Ra-am-ses to Suc-coth . . . *Exodus* 12:37.

As long as no historical evidence existed to establish the whereabouts of Goshen, the Hyksos capital Avaris or the treasure (store) cities of Pithom and Ramses, the biblical story of Joseph was the subject of two opposing views. Some, including the Church, saw it as a strictly factual account of events: others dismissed it as simply a collection of legendary tales. New light began to be thrown on the matter, however, when Egypt started to recover memory of its distant past at the start of the last century after Jean François Champollion (1790–1832), a brilliant young French scientist, had completed the final deciphering of the hieroglyphic section of the Rosetta Stone. The stone, which is thought to have originated from a temple, came to light when an expeditionary force led by Napoleon Bonaparte was repairing fortifications to the north of Rasheed on the left bank of the Nile in the western delta. Champollion's work aroused great interest in Egyptian antiquities among Europeans, plus considerable hope that it would be possible at last to find in Egypt confirmation of the story of the Israelites' Descent and the Exodus. It also inspired an international assault upon the treasures from Egypt's past.

One of the first plunderers was a bizarre and flamboyant Italian, Giovanni Belzoni, a student of hydraulics who was, physically, a giant—six feet seven inches tall, broad of shoulder and enormously powerful. He worked as a strong man at Sadler's Wells Theatre in

London and in circuses before moving to Egypt with the intention of selling hydraulic machinery for irrigation purposes. When this project proved unsuccessful, he turned his energies to the collection of antiquities by the simple means of tomb-robbing. In 1817, Belzoni was employed by Henry Salt, the British Consul-General in Egypt, to remove the colossal bust of Ramses II, later to be housed in the British Museum along with other valuable pieces, from Thebes. Subsequently he joined an excavation at Karnak, and it was he, in fact, who discovered the tomb of Aye, who sat on the Egyptian throne for a short period after the death of Tutankhamun. Later still he was to be found among the tombs at Thebes where he opened six in all, the most famous of which was that of Seti I, the father of Ramses II. The latter was a figure of great significance to biblical scholars, who had long identified him with the un-named Pharaoh of the Jewish Oppression.

Belzoni, a clumsy operator who did much damage, was followed by a scholar much better equipped for the task—the German archaeologist Karl Lepsius (1810–1884), who is accepted as the greatest in his field after Champollion. Between 1842 and 1845 he led a Prussian expedition, which included several skilled draughtsmen among its members and is recognised as the best-equipped team ever sent to Egypt. Lepsius excavated the site of the Fayyum Labyrynth, a Ramesside construction in Middle Egypt, before travelling south to Khartoum in the Sudan and then to the Sinai desert in the north-east. His exhaustive work can be measured by the fact that he was able to send home 15,000 Egyptian antiquities and plaster casts. His most valuable service to students of Egyptology, however, was his compilation *Denkmäler*, probably the largest opus of Egyptian scholarship ever produced, in which he collected and translated Egyptian texts. After Lepsius, another rather curious figure appeared on the scene—this time from France—in the shape of François Mariette Pasha, a native of Boulogne, who was sent out from Paris by the Louvre in 1850 to collect Coptic manuscripts. Mariette never returned to the Louvre, but accepted instead the newly-created post of head of the Egyptian Service of Antiquities in Cairo. Mariette worked in Egypt for thirty years, during which he dug in thirty-five sites, ranging from Aswan in the south to the Mediterranean. Among his important discoveries were the famous statue of Ramses II and monuments of the same king excavated at Tanis in the eastern delta. In his desire to clear as many monuments as possible, Mariette used crude methods, for which he was much criticised by later archaeologists. He was even said to have dynamited the fallen ruins of a temple while excavating near the Sphinx. Little of his immense work was ever published, for, in his search for imposing monuments and precious objects, Mariette had a fatal habit of ignoring small, but historically valuable, finds. He has his place in history, however, for four reasons: his creation of the first National Antiquities Service in Egypt; the foundation of the first Cairo Museum in 1859; the fact that he put·an end to the sacking of ancient sites, and that he refused to allow any further exportation of antiquities from Egypt.

The high hopes that Egypt would provide historical proof of the Joseph story and the relationship between the Israelites and the land of the Pharaohs seemed to have come nearer to fulfilment. Up to that time Egypt had been able to provide only confirmation of details of the biblical narrations of Joseph and the Exodus such as locations, phrases, expressions, customs, titles and proper nouns, and only one mention of Israel has been found. This was on the Israel Stele of King Merenptah, discovered by Flinders Petrie at Thebes in 1896 and now in Cairo Museum. The stele relates to a period not later than the fifth year of the king's reign and, after a lengthy song celebrating the triumphs of his victories in Libya and Palestine, ends with these words: 'Canaan is captured with every evil circumstance. Askalon is carried captive. Gezer is taken. Yenoam is brought to nought. Israel is destroyed, its seed is not. Syria has become as the widow of Egypt. All the lands together are at peace.'

Britain finally appeared on the scene in the last quarter of the nineteenth century. The first British archaeological mission, led by Henri Naville, the Swiss Egyptologist and biblical scholar, arrived at the start of the winter of 1883—a year after the Egypt Exploration Fund (the name was changed later to the Egypt Exploration Society) had been established in London—to work at Tell el-Maskhuta in the eastern delta. Their specific hope was to confirm that a site visited by Lepsius, who had not excavated in the area but had merely recorded what he saw, was one of the store cities, Pithom. Six months later, Naville explained to the Fund's first annual general meeting: 'On the south bank of the Sweet Water Canal, which runs from Cairo to Suez, stand the ruins of a few European-style houses, now quite abandoned, but which only a few years ago were a flourishing village. The French called it Ramesses, it having first been named thus by Lepsius. The

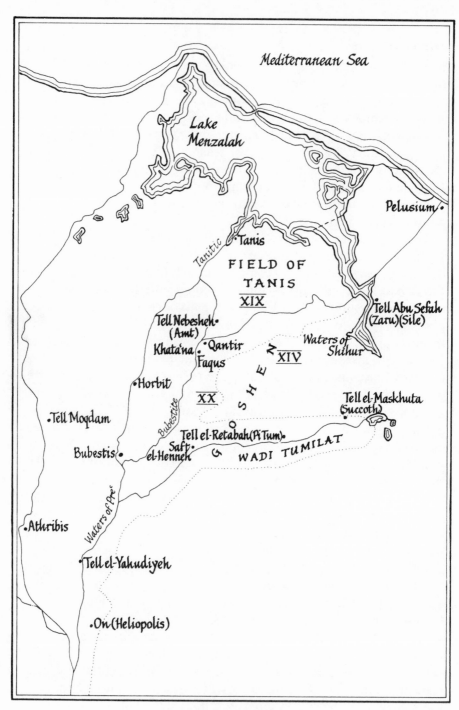

The Eastern Delta

name is derived from a large monolith, which represents a king sitting between two gods and was the only monument visible above the sand when Lepsius visited the place in 1866. He recognised two of the figures at once as those of the gods Re and Tum, later identifying the third as that of Ramses II. Supposing that the monolith was part of a sanctuary, he concluded that the place must have been called Pa, the abode of Ramses, and that it was one of the biblical store cities constructed by the Israelites at the time of the Oppression. This theory . . . had many arguments in its favour and . . . (this site) was therefore selected as the starting-point of the work of the first season.'

Naville went on to explain how, a few years after Lepsius's visit, a party of French engineers became engaged in constructing the Suez Canal and settled in the area. While digging the foundations of one of the houses, they came across another monolith, exactly similar to the first and placed just opposite so as to form the other side of an entrance. When they dug further, two sphinxes with human heads were also found, as well as a large granite tablet, engraved on both sides, and what appeared to be a sanctuary of a temple. Naville went on: 'What struck me chiefly was that all these monuments were dedicated to the god Tum Harmakhis, especially the naos, or sanctuary, which contains a sphinx with a human head, a well-known form of the god Harmakhis. Hence it was to be expected that the excavations would show that the city, although built by Ramses II, was not called "the abode of Ramses" but "the abode of Tum"—that is, Pi Tum or Pithom.

'I had therefore a definite question to solve: Was Tell el-Maskhuta actually Pithom or was it Ramses? Should I find the abode of Tum or, according to Lepsius's theory, should I find the abode of Ramses? On looking at some stones which the men had uncovered, I found one which bore some hieroglyphics. It was a tablet, the top of which was defaced. Only the last lines were legible, and seemed to contain a decree concerning a statue. Four days later another piece was found, the lower part of the statue of a standing man, the top of which had been broken off, and on the back were three lines of hieroglyphs giving his titles: "The chief of the Storehouse, the scribe of the abode of Tum, of Succoth. Hathor grants that thy name may remain with this statue in the abode of Tum, the great living god of Succoth." Subsequently the men found two more fragments of a very pretty head in red granite. On digging further they found two parts of the statue of a squatting man with his hands crossed over his knees. He was a man holding very high office in the time of the Twentieth Dynasty king (Osorkon II, a successor of Shishank). Among his titles is "The good recorder of Pithom (Pi Tum)".'

Naville went on: 'Let us now continue for a moment the history of the city of Pithom. There is not the slightest doubt that the founder of the city is the king of the Oppression, Ramses II. There are no names more ancient than his on the monuments and there are no traces of any sovereign of an earlier date. Before him there may have existed a sanctuary for the god Tum, but certainly it was he who built the enclosure and the store-chambers. All those walls belong to the very best period of Egyptian brick-building and, although I never had the good fortune to find the king's name stamped on any of the bricks, they are exactly similar to those found so-stamped in other parts of Egypt. I may add that some of them are made with straw or with fragments of reed, of which traces are still to be seen, and some are mere Nile mud without any straw at all.' Naville was trying to prove that the bricks he found were the same kind as those made by the Israelites while building the two store cities for Pharaoh. Although they used straw at first, the supply ran out:

> And the taskmasters of the people went out, and their officers, and they spake to the people, saying, Thus saith Pharaoh, I will not give you straw. Go ye, get you straw where ye can find it: yet not ought of your work shall be diminished. *Exodus* 5:10, 11.

Naville then concluded: 'Since it is proved that Ramses II was the founder of Pithom, we have, as you may see, the strongest reason possible to believe that we have at last found one of the Exodus cities, and that these are the very bricks which caused the Israelites so much suffering and distress.'

Tell el-Maskhuta is situated in the Wadi Tumilat, a shallow valley about thirty miles long, bordered by desert on either side and connecting the Egyptian delta with Lake Timsah in the canal area. Naville's statement that it was one of the store cities caused great satisfaction for biblical scholars of the time although his views have since been subjected to some revision. In 1918 Alan Gardiner showed that, although Tell el-Maskhuta was a city of the god Tum, it was not the main city. He identified Pithom with another Wadi Tumilat city, west of Tell el-Maskhuta, called Tell el-Retabah. It was the German philologist Emil Brugsch who subsequently suggested that Tell el-Maskhuta, known from Egyptian inscriptions as *tkw*, was not one of the store cities but the biblical Succoth, the first stop on the Israelites' journey at the time of the Exodus. As for Goshen, the translators of the Greek Septuagint related it, too, to the Wadi Timulat and, in particular, the town of Heroonopolis, the ancient name for Tell el-Maskhuta. The Septuagint says:

> And he (Jacob) sent Judah before them to Joseph to meet him at Heroonopolis. *Genesis* 46: 28, 29.

More recently, Henri Naville showed that the name Goshen is to be found in an Egyptian town called Faqus, whose ancient name he read as *gsm* (the Egyptian *s* is read as *sh* in Hebrew while the *m* is read as *n*). *Gsm*, echoing the distant words of Josephus, was situated on the Bubestite eastern branch of the Nile in the delta. It was the chief city of the twentieth nome—known as the Arabian nome—which included the Wadi Tumilat area.

There is now general agreement among scholars that Goshen is an area in the eastern delta, bounded by the Bubestite branch of the Nile, with Faqus—its governing city—to the north-west, Tell el-Retabah (Pithom) to the south and Tell el-Maskhuta (Succoth) to the south-east. This branch of the river flows north-east through On (Heliopolis) to Qantir, then east through Sile to Pelusium. Some maps refer to the stretch of the river after Qantir as the Pelusiac branch, but Ptolemy of Alexandria makes it clear in the book about Egyptian geography which he wrote in AD 150 that the whole length of the river, from south of On to Pelusium, was considered to be the Bubestite branch.

The site of the city of Pi-Ramses, where the Exodus is believed to have started, has proved more elusive, however. It has been accepted for many years that it was on the same site as the Hyksos capital Avaris because both cities share the same description of their general neighbourhoods and geographical features, such as rivers and nomes. Many scholars have, in addition, identified Avaris and Pi-Ramses with Zoan, the place where Moses is said to have performed wonders against the Egyptians:

> Marvellous things did he in the sight of their fathers, in the land of Egypt, in the field of Zoan. He divided the sea, and caused them to pass through; and he made the waters to stand as an heap. *Psalm* 78:12, 13.

Zoan of the Bible is known to have been the ancient city of Za'ne, called Tanis by the Greeks and the modern San el-Hagar on Lake Menzalah at the end of the Tanitic branch of the Nile in the delta. Alan Gardiner was one eminent scholar who accepted Tanis as the site of Avaris and Ramses, despite the fact that it was situated in the nineteenth Egyptian nome whereas Avaris was in the fourteenth. This geographical discrepancy caused him to dismiss Tanis initially, but he subsequently changed his mind, partly because of the discovery by Pierre Montet, the French archaeologist and scholar, that 'the gods of Pi-Ramses were really the gods of Tanis', partly because of the rich remains—stelae, statues of gods and kings, obelisks as well as parts of buildings—found there. The claims of Tanis were also reinforced by the fact that the biblical narrator chose to make a point of the time when the city was built:

> And they ascended by the south, and came unto He-bron . . .
> (Now He-bron was built seven years before Zo-an in Egypt.)
> *Numbers* 13:22.

However, remains of the Ramesside period have been found all over the eastern delta, leading scholars to champion a variety of other places as the correct site of Pi-Ramses. Naville, for instance, favoured Khata'na Qantir, a district a few miles north-west of Faqus on the Bubestite branch of the Nile, where discoveries included the remains of a palace of Ramses II with splendid faience tiles, a base of a colossus of the same king, stelae and a well inscribed with Ramses II's name. Qantir, like Tanis, poses a geographical difficulty as the site of Pi-Ramses, however, because it, too, is in a different nome from Avaris, the twentieth. Nevertheless Naville's conclusions caused Alan Gardiner to modify, although not entirely abandon, his opinion again in 1961, in his book *Egypt of the Pharaohs*, where he admitted that Qantir is a possible alternative to Tanis: 'Among other scholars Labib Habachi has been particularly active and successful in finding stelae and other evidence from the same neighbourhood, which might swing the pendulum in that direction. According to this theory, the monuments of Ramses II at Tanis were transported there by the kings of the Twenty-first Dynasty, who are known to have chosen that city as their capital. The debate continues, and cannot be regarded as having been settled.'

It is my belief that neither Tanis, Qantir nor most of the other places suggested in the past are the correct location for the Exodus city of Pi-Ramses. Avaris and Pi-Ramses—as well as the fortress Zaru where Joseph is thought to have been imprisoned—are to be found in the fourteenth nome at Tell Abu Sefah, on the north-east fringes of Goshen and near the modern frontier town of Kantarah, which had—and still has—a bridge that has to be crossed by any Egyptian troops entering Palestine by the route across the north of the peninsula of Sinai.

Scholars are not in dispute about the precise location of Zaru, which was the starting point of Palestinian and Syrian campaigns mentioned from the time of Tuthmosis III (c.1490–1436 BC), the Eighteenth Dynasty ruler, right through to the time of Seti I, the second king of the Nineteenth Dynasty, and his successors, Ramses II and Ramses III. The only question of consequence therefore is to examine the evidence that links it with Pi-Ramses, which was in its turn built upon the same site as Avaris.

In the account of Manetho, as given by Josephus, we are told that Avaris was 'in the Sethroite nome' and 'situated on the east of the Bubestite branch of the Nile'. The Kamose Stele, with its reference to 'the wine of your vineyard' and cutting down trees, suggests that it was a fertile area and that the city had a harbour suitable for a large number of ships. This is elaborated upon by Ahmose, son of Abana, in his story of the siege of Avaris by Ahmosis I in which he describes how the Egyptian forces reached the area by water to arrive south of Avaris and conduct the fighting while on the water. This makes it clear that Avaris was situated on the bank of a lake or pond, connected with the branches of the Nile to the east of the delta and large enough for the movement of ships. As we saw earlier, it was also the main centre from Hyksos times for the worship of the god Seth (Sutekh).

What do we know about Pi-Ramses? When this city appears, it is usually related to Ramses II—*pi-Ramsses-myr-Amun* (House-of-Ramses-Beloved-of-Amun). Although many cities in the delta, and even in Egypt as a whole, are related to one of the Ramses kings, this Pi-Ramses was recognised as the residence of the Ramesside kings in the delta, and scholars usually speak of its having been established by Ramses II. The evidence points, however, to the city already being in existence when he came to the throne. The inscriptions he had made on the walls of the temple of his father, Seti I, at Abydos in Upper Egypt give an account of a visit Ramses II made in the first year of his reign to

Thebes to attend the festival of Amun (Pharaohs were usually crowned at Memphis, near present-day Cairo in Lower Egypt). When the festival has ended, Ramses mentions that he 'set sail . . . and directed his face downstream to the mighty place, House-of-Ramses-Beloved-of-Amun-Great-of-Victories'. Alan Gardiner commented (*The Journal of Egyptian Archaeology*, 1918) that this reference 'forms, therefore, excellent evidence that Pi-Ramses was the northern capital at this date (year 1 of Ramses II)'.

Evidence that the fortress of Zaru and the House of Ramses were in the same locality is provided by the triumphal poem, known as the *Poem of Pentaur*, recording Ramses II's victories in Syria and Palestine in the fifth year of his reign. It begins like this: 'Year 5, second month of summer, day 9, His Majesty passed the fortress of Zaru . . . (a description of the king's appearance follows) . . . now when many days had passed over these things, His Majesty being in the town of Ramses-Beloved-of-Amun . . .' The story goes on to describe the king's journey northward to Palestine.

This is by no means the end of the corroborative evidence. In the Papyrus Anastasi, which dates from the Ramesside period, there is a letter from two officers in the army of the Royal Butler in which they state that they have set forth from the place where Pharaoh was (probably Memphis) and, in accordance with the orders of the king (Ramses II), were bringing with them three stelae. They report that they have just passed the frontier fortress Zaru where they were about to unload their vessels at the 'Dwelling-of-Ramses-Beloved-of-Amun'. From this position, they explain, the monuments will have to be dragged to their desired resting place, and they ask the Royal Butler to send new instructions. The geographical position of Zaru—and, with it, Avaris and Pi-Ramses—as a frontier fortress is also confirmed in Papyrus Anastasi where it is described as: 'The forefront of every foreign land, the end of Egypt.'

Papyrus Anastasi also gives a description of Pi-Ramses: 'It is a fair spot, there is not the like of it, resembling Thebes. It was Re who founded it himself. The residence is agreeable to live in, its fields are full of all good things; it is furnished with abundant provisions every day; its backwaters are full of fishes and its pools of birds; its meads are verdant with herbage, the greenery is a cubit and a half in height, the fruit is like the taste of honey in the cultivated fields; its granaries . . . draw near to the sky; onions and leeks . . . clusters of flowers in the grove; pomegranates, apples and olives; figs from the orchard; sweet vine of Kenkeme surpassing honey; red *wd*-fish from the lake of the residence . . . The Waters-of-Horus (Shi-Hur) yield salt and *phr natron* (a chemical used in mummification). Its ships fare forth and return to port. Abundance of food is in it every day: one rejoiceth to dwell within it, no wish is left to be spoken. The small in it is like the great.'[1]

The Waters of Shi-Hur would seem to be Lake Ballah, south of Zaru, which was connected to the Pelusiac end of the Bubestite branch of the Nile. Thus ships coming from Thebes could sail all the way to the harbour of Zaru, close to the Palestine border, and, in the case of army units, it was only there that they had to start their campaigns on foot. This lake must also be the pleasure lake mentioned in the last of Amenhotep III's five scarabs: 'Year 11, third month of the first season, day 1, under the majesty of . . . Amenhotep III, given life; and the Great King's-Wife Tiye, in her city of Zarukha. Its length is 3,700 cubits; its width 700 cubits. His majesty celebrated the feast of the lake, in the third month of the first season, day 16, when his majesty sailed thereon in the Royal barge *Aten Gleams*.' It was John H. Breasted who decided to read the name without the final sign for *kha*, which he took to imply a city. This left him with the city of Zarw (Zaru), *t3r-w*,[2] the same name as the fortress. The story of Zaru is therefore that it was an Egyptian frontier fortress from the time of the Twelfth Dynasty when it was called the Pathes of Horus. It was later rebuilt by the Hyksos kings with strong walls and became known as Avaris. After the expulsion of the Hyksos, it was used as a frontier fortress and prison by the kings of the Eighteenth Dynasty, during whose reigns it started to be known as Zaru. When Joseph's Israelite family came to Egypt, in order not to allow them into Egypt proper Amenhotep III gave the city of Zaru to his queen, Tiye, and her Asiatic shepherd relations. On becoming king after the Amarna rebellion,

---

[1] *Zeitschrift für Ägyptische Sprache*, G. Steindorff.

[2] As the Egyptian sign for 'r' is the same as that for 'l', we can also read the name of the city as Zalw. C. Kuthman, the German philologist, confirmed that this was also the Coptic city named Sele or Sile, corresponding to Tell Abu Sefah near Kantarah. The name of Tiye's city at the time of the Romans was read as Sele or Zele. If we were to read the full name in Amenhotep III's scarab, using the vowels of the Coptic period, it becomes Zelekha, the very same name included in Islamic traditions and the Jewish Talmud.

Horemheb turned the city back into a prison under the mayorship of
Ramses, later to become Ramses I, who established the Nineteenth
Dynasty. It was then that it was rebuilt and received its biblical name,
Pi-Ramses, from its mayor. The city eventually became the northern
residence of the first three kings of the Nineteenth Dynasty,
Rames I, Seti I and Ramses II, who embellished the name.

The significance of this restoration has been clouded by the 400-year
stele, originally discovered at Tanis by Mariette. This stele was issued
by Ramses II, in the third decade of his long reign, to honour the
anniversary of four centuries of rule by the god Seth at Avaris, which
had occurred some time before he came to the throne. The four
centuries, allied to the delay in issuing the stele, dovetail neatly with
two of the biblical references to the length of the sojourn—four
centuries and four hundred and thirty years—and this, plus the fact
that Ramses is the only Pharaonic name we find in the Pentateuch, has
provided an irresistibly easy option for supporters of the Hyksos-to-
Ramses II theory. It is certainly true that the memory of the Israelites
would not have insisted on the name Ramses without strong reason,
but the 400-year stele should be interpreted in a different way from the
conventional one. What it makes clear is that, in mentioning Ramses,
the biblical narrator is not departing from the normal practice and
using Pharaoh's name: he is referring to the period during the reign of
Horemheb when Ramses II's grandfather, also named Ramses, and
Ramses II's father, Seti, were mayors and viziers of Avaris.

The stele reads: 'Live the Horus, Mighty Bull, Who Loves Truth
(Ramses II) . . . His majesty commanded the making of a great stele of
granite bearing the name of his fathers, in order to set up the name of
the father of his fathers (the god Seth) (and of) the King Menmaat-Re,
the Son of Re: Seti Mern-Ptah, enduring and abiding for ever like Re
every day. Year 400, 4th month of the third season, day 4, of the King
of Upper and Lower Egypt: Seth-the-Great-of-Strength, the Son of Re,
his beloved; The-Ombite, beloved of Re-Harakhti, so that he exists
forever and ever. Now there came the Hereditary Prince, Mayor of the
City and Vizier, Fan-Bearer on the Right Hand of the King, Troop
Commander, Overseer of Foreign Countries, Overseer of the Fortress
of Zaru, Chief of Police, Royal Scribe, Master of Horse, Conductor of
the Feast of the Ram-the-Lord of Mendes, High Priest of Seth and
Overseer of the Prophets of All the Gods; Seti, the triumphant, the son
of the hereditary prince (Ramses, who later became Ramses I), Mayor

of the City and Vizier, Troop Commander, Overseer of Foreign Countries, Overseer of the Fortress of Zaru, Royal Scribe and Master of Horse, Pa-Ramses, the triumphant, the child of the Lady of the House . . .'

Ramses I was very old when he ascended to the throne as founder of the Nineteenth Dynasty and he ruled for only a couple of years before being succeeded by his son as Seti I. He must therefore have been mayor of Avaris for a long time. Ramses II also served as mayor of Avaris when he was a crown prince and was probably born in the city. All the indications are that it was the Ramses mayors who forced the Israelites to build the store cities in the Goshen area as well as rebuilding Zaru itself which, as we saw earlier, was already Pi-Ramses, the delta residence of Ramses II, in the very first year of his reign—and, like Rome, it cannot have been built in a day. Finally, to return to the starting point of this chapter . . .

There is no suggestion anywhere that the Israelites ever moved from the place where they first settled, Goshen in the eastern delta. The whole story of their banishment to a remote region where they would not give offence to the Egyptians consequently makes sense only if they arrived in the country when the seat of power was at Thebes, the better part of four hundred miles away. As for their proximity to the Royal residence at the time when Moses was born, this is simply explained: it was the kings, not the Israelites, who moved. The later rulers of the Eighteenth Dynasty made their capital in the delta instead of Thebes—Tutankhamun, for instance, spent most of his life at Memphis—and finally, as we saw above, the first three kings of the Nineteenth Dynasty, Ramses I, Seti I and Ramses II, made Zaru, now called Pi-Ramses, their northern residence.

The one important question remaining is: How long did the Israelites' sojourn in Egypt last—four centuries or four generations?

Chapter 11

SOJOURN

The contradictory accounts given in the Old Testament about the length of time the Israelites spent in Egypt are one of the reasons that have misled scholars into accepting the Hyksos period as the right time for Joseph's appearance in the country. The relevant texts are:

> . . . Know of a surety that thy seed shall be a stranger in a land that is not theirs, and shall serve them; and they shall afflict them four hundred years . . . But in the fourth generation they shall come hither again. *Genesis* 15:13, 16.

> Now the sojourning of the children of Israel, who dwelt in Egypt, was four hundred and thirty years. *Exodus* 12:40.

To turn to the actual Hebrew, Abraham was warned that his descendants would dwell in a foreign land for *arba' m3wt shana* (four hundred years) and Exodus confirms this figure by stating that the sojourn of the children of Israel was *shalsheem shana wa arb' m3wt shana* (thirty years and four hundred years). On the other hand, Genesis also says *wa dor rabi'i yashwbw hena* (and the fourth generation return they here). More than a century ago, in his book *Historical and Critical Commentary on the Old Testament*, the biblical scholar M. M. Kalisch tried to explain this discrepancy by saying that the age of those generations was to be looked upon as one hundred and twenty years: 'The "fourth generation" after the settlement of Jacob in Egypt was promised to be led back to Palestine. Unless we suppose these words contain an obvious discrepancy, the "four generations" must embrace a period of more than four hundred years; and no alternative is left but to understand here that term *dor* as the duration of life which, as a general rule, was allotted to man after the deluge.'

More recently, K. A. Kitchen of Liverpool University tried to use the evidence of the Ugaritic tablets found in northern Syria early this century to give a different meaning to the Hebrew word *dor*. 'Abraham is told that his descendants will re-enter Canaan in "the fourth generation",' he argued in his book *The Ancient Orient and the Old Testament*. 'The simplest explanation is that the four *dor* correspond to the four hundred years, not to "generations" in the modern sense. This is suggested not by a mere wish for harmonisation, but by perfectly clear evidence from Ugaritic and early Assyrian sources that *dor* or *daru* can mean a "span" or "cycle of time" of eighty years or more.'[1]

This argument is quite unsound for a variety of reasons. For example, the Hebrew verse did not say, as Dr Kitchen did, that Abraham's descendants would re-enter Canaan in the fourth (*dor*); the translation is: 'And the fourth (*dor*) return they here.' It is therefore 'the fourth dor' that is the subject of the verb. In this case, *dor* can only mean 'generation', which, in fact, is also confirmed by the Ugaritic texts to which Dr Kitchen refers.[2] There is not one example in them, or in Hebrew or Assyrian texts, where the word *dor* was used to mean a hundred-year cycle, but if, as Dr Kitchen insists, the word *dor* in this case means a span or cycle of time of eighty years or more, how much more? Could it go for an unspecified, unlimited length of time so that four hundred years might be just one cycle? However, the basic objection to Dr Kitchen's theory is that he does not seem to realise that when the word *dor* is used to mean a cycle of time it has the sense of a 'turn', in which case the length of a single turn must be given at the start. This is not the case in Genesis.

What confirms that the biblical word *dor* is used to mean 'a generation' is the fact that the Pentateuch names only four generations between the time of the Descent into Egypt and the subsequent Exodus. In the list of Jacob and his descendants who went down to Egypt we have:

And the sons of Levi: Ger-shon, Ko-hath and Me-rar-i ...
Genesis 46:11.

[1] In his view, the extra thirty years mentioned in Exodus do not conflict with this theory: 'The four hundred years is a round figure in prospect, while the four hundred and thirty is more precise in retrospect.'
[2] *Ugaritic Manual, III,* Cyrus H. Gordon.

After the arrival in Egypt, Levi had a daughter:

> And the name of Amram's wife was Joch-e-bed, the daughter of
> Levi, whom her mother bare to Levi in Egypt . . . *Numbers* 26:59.

The fact that Jochebed was Levi's daughter is confirmed in the Book of
Exodus:

> And the sons of Ko-hath (were) Amram, and Iz-har, and He-bron
> and Uz-zi-el . . . And Amram took him Joch-e-bed his father's
> sister, to wife; and she bare him Aaron and Moses . . . *Exodus*
> 6:18, 20.

Obviously, this genealogy cannot possibly add up to four hundred and
thirty years. In fact, the genealogy of the Pentateuch is constantly in
disagreement with an Israelite sojourn of more than four centuries.
Two of Moses' cousins, for example, make their appearance in the
story of the Exodus—Elizaphan, the son of Uzziel, and Korah, the son
of Izhar:

> And the chief of the house of the father of the families of the
> Ko-hath-ites shall be E-li-za-phan, the son of Uz-zi-el. *Numbers*
> 3:30.

> Now Kor-ah, the son of Iz-har, the son of Ko-hath, the son of Levi
> . . . took men; And they rose up before Moses with certain of the
> children of Israel. *Numbers* 16:1, 2.

Another example is Makir, the grandson of Joseph from Manasseh,
who is said to have been alive not only at the time of the Exodus but
when Joshua later conquered Canaan:

> And Moses gave Gilead unto Mach-ir, the son of Ma-nas-seh; and
> they dwelt therein. *Numbers* 32:40.

As Moses was the great-grandson of Levi, Joseph's elder brother, it is
even possible that Joseph was still alive at the time when Moses was
born.

Apart from the scholastic arguments involved, anyone who is
familiar with the Near and Middle East would instinctively prefer four
generations to four centuries as the time of the Israelites' sojourn in
Egypt. It is possible even today, for instance, to find Bedouins who can
tell you all about their great-great-great-great-grandfather but do not

know the date of their own birth, which they have to invent should they find themselves requiring a passport.[1]

A few scholars like Cyrus H. Gordon, the American biblical and Egyptian scholar who translated the Ugaritic texts, H. H. Rowley and Bowman have used genealogical records to try to decide the length of time that elapsed between Jacob's arrival in Egypt and the birth of Moses, and have also noted that the Oppression in Egypt is not represented in the Bible as lasting anything like four hundred and thirty years: immediately after Joseph's death at the end of the Book of Genesis, we are given the story of 'the king who knew not Joseph' and the birth of Moses at the beginning of the Book of Exodus. How then did the biblical editor, working some time between the fifth and third centuries BC, arrive at the figure of four hundred and thirty years?

It seems to me that it is the result of three mathematical calculations on his part. Firstly, with no one to turn to for help, he added up the ages of the four generations as they are given in the Old Testament.

Levi	137	(*Exodus* 6:16)
Kohath	133	(*Exodus* 6:18)
Amram	137	(*Exodus* 6:20)
Moses	120	(*Deuteronomy* 34:7)

This gave him a total of five hundred and twenty-seven years. He then added together Levi's age at the time of the Descent, which he fixed arbitrarily at fifty-seven, and the forty years that Moses lived after the Exodus. This provided a second total of ninety-seven years, the time that Levi and Moses lived outside of Egypt. Subtracting the second total from the first left him with a final figure of four hundred and thirty years.

If the Israelite sojourn in Egypt lasted only four generations, about a century, as the evidence seems to me clearly to indicate, and we go back a century for an Exodus at the start of the Nineteenth Dynasty (c.1306 BC), we arrive at the time of Tuthmosis IV (c.1413–1405 BC), who appointed Yuya as his vizier. To summarise what I believe to be the correct sequence of events . . .

Abram and Sarai made their initial journey down to Egypt at the

---

[1] The Talmud does not agree with 430 years as the length of the Israelites' sojourn in Egypt: 'And the children of Israel journeyed from Raamses to Succoth. Two hundred and ten years after their entrance into Egypt, the Israelites departed therefrom, six hundred thousand men, with wives and children.'—*Selections from the Talmud*, translated by H. Polano.

time, more than a century after the end of the Hyksos rule, when
Tuthmosis III (c.1490–1436 BC), the sixth king of the Eighteenth
Dynasty, was on the throne. It was he who married Sarai and fathered
Isaac, the son born to her after the couple had returned to Canaan.
On the death of Isaac, the elder of his twin sons, Esau, sold his
birthright—the title as a prince of Egypt—cheaply to the younger one,
Jacob, from whom it passed to his son, Joseph. It was Tuthmosis IV
(c.1413–1405 BC), the eighth king of the Eighteenth Dynasty, in
residence at Thebes and ruling over the precise area—from the Nile to
Euphrates—referred to in the promise to Abraham about his seed,
who appointed Joseph as his vizier after he had been sold into slavery
in Egypt and had successfully interpreted the king's dreams. The king
invited Joseph's family to settle in Egypt and offered them land at
Goshen in the eastern delta, remote from the court, a frontier region
which, as Alan Gardiner has put it, was already used to 'an infiltration
by Palestinians glad to find refuge in a more peaceful and fertile
environment'. Joseph and his wife continued to serve Amenhotep III,
the next Pharaoh, who broke with Egyptian tradition and, although he
married his sister, instead of making her his queen, married and gave
the title to Joseph's daughter, Tiye. He also gave her the fortress of
Zaru, the former Avaris of the Hyksos, dominating the land of Goshen
where her Israelite ancestors were allowed to settle, as her own city.
Three of Tiye's descendants—Amenhotep IV (Akhnaten), Semenkhkare and Tutankhamun—followed on the throne, to be succeeded in
their turn by Joseph's own son, Aye. Then came Horemheb, the last
ruler of the Eighteenth Dynasty, the 'king who knew not Joseph', who
turned against the Israelites, set them to the harsh work of building the
store cities of Pithom and Pi-Ramses in the Goshen region under the
mayorship of Ramses and his son, Seti, restored Zaru to its former
position as a fortress prison and, at the end of four Israelite generations
in Egypt, prompted the Exodus. I believe that this actually took place
during the following brief reign of Ramses I.

My argument for this chronology is supported by the agreement of
both biblical and historical evidence on the length of the reign of the
king of the Exodus. The death of the oppressor king is reported as
follows:

> And it came to pass in process of time, that the king of Egypt died:
> and the children of Israel sighed under the bondage . . . *Exodus*
> 2:23.

And the Lord said unto Moses in Midian, Go, return into Egypt: for all the men are dead which sought thy life. *Exodus* 4:19.

It is after this that Moses starts his mission to lead the Israelites out of Egypt:

Come now therefore (God tells Moses), and I will send thee unto Pharaoh, that thou mayest bring forth my people the children of Israel out of Egypt. *Exodus* 3:10.

This Pharaoh must be the one who followed the death of the oppressor king and, if we accept that Horemheb was the oppressor, the new king can only be Ramses I. It was this king whom Moses met:

. . . Moses and Aaron went in, and told Pharaoh, Thus saith the Lord God of Israel, Let my people go . . . *Exodus* 5:1.

According to the Bible, 'Moses was fourscore years old, and Aaron was fourscore and three years old, when they spake unto Pharaoh.' (*Exodus* 7:7.) The new king refused to allow the Israelites to leave, and there followed a series of catastrophes which, by their nature, must have taken four seasons to occur. Then Pharaoh agreed to let them go, and they started their journey from the city of Rameses (*Exodus* 12:37), the native city of Ramses I. They were pursued by Pharaoh who was eventually drowned in the sea (*Exodus* 14:28).

If we take the biblical account here to be accurate, the new king must have died before the end of his second year on the throne. From historical evidence, we know this to be the case in respect of Ramses I.

Chapter 12

DOPPELGÄNGER

If the biblical Joseph and the historical Yuya are the same person, it must be possible to fit them into the same chronology. It was suggested in an earlier chapter that, on the evidence available, Yuya must have been born between 1453/2 and 1439/38 BC and died some time between 1393/2 and 1379/78 BC. Although we do not, as a rule, accept biblical figures and ages without corroborative evidence, the age of thirty that the Bible gives to Joseph at the time of his appointment as vizier seems reasonable, taking into account the fact that he was sold into Egypt, served for a time in Potiphar's house and was in prison for some years. If we accept the age as accurate, and if Tuthmosis IV (c.1413–1405 BC) was the Pharaoh who made him his vizier, we arrive at a birth date of 1443 to 1435 BC.

This leaves a span of from 46 to 54 years between the earliest year that Tuthmosis III, who was already a married adult occupying a priestly office when he came to the throne, could have fathered Isaac, and the birth of Joseph. Into those years we have to make allowance for Isaac growing up and fathering Esau and Jacob who, in his turn, had ten sons and a daughter by three different wives before Joseph was born. The possible span is adequate for these events in an era when people married and became parents at an early age. For example, the first of the fourteen Pharaohs of the Eighteenth Dynasty, Ahmosis, came to the throne c.1575 BC and the last, Horemheb, c.1335 BC, a total of two hundred and forty years. If we take away both Hatshepsut, who ruled together with her stepson, Tuthmosis III, and Semenkhkare, who was co-regent with Akhnaten, the average is only twenty years. There is also evidence that Isaac married when exceptionally young, perhaps fourteen, the age of adulthood. He was still a boy when the angel of the Lord stopped Abraham's intended sacrifice —'Lay not thine hand upon the boy' (*Genesis* 22:12)—and there are conflicting views about whether it was fear over her husband's intentions or joy at learning he had changed his mind that brought about Sarah's death. However, when it comes to Isaac's own marriage to Rebekah, we are told: 'And Isaac brought her into his mother Sarah's tent, and took Rebekah, and she became his wife; and he loved her; and Isaac was comforted after his mother's death' (*Genesis* 24:67).[1]

It is impossible to examine the lives of Joseph and Yuya without also being struck by the remarkable number of similarities between them.

THEIR NAMES

The only known reference to Yuya before the discovery of his tomb was in the scarab issued by Amenhotep III in celebration of his marriage to Yuya's daughter, Tiye. It seems the king wanted everyone to know the name of the woman he had made his queen against the customs of his country. Copies were sent to foreign princes, reading in part '. . . the Great King's-Wife Tiye, who liveth. The name of her father is Yuya, the name of her mother is Tuya . . .' It was only then that the identity of Tiye's parents became known: earlier she had been thought to be a Mesopotamian princess from Mitanni, sent to Egypt to marry the king.

Only four letters were used by the scribes and craftsmen who wrote Yuya's name on the objects in his tomb:

 alef   phonetic value A

 alef or *yodh*   phonetic value A or Y

 yodh   phonetic value Y

 waw   phonetic value W

There was a fifth sign, called a determinative, that has no phonetic value and is merely inserted to help us to understand the meaning. In this particular case it indicates that the preceding letters are to be read as a man's name. Although only four signs were used, the result was a pronounced variation in the way Yuya's name was spelled. In all there are eleven spellings:

---

[1] Genesis, characteristically, also tells us that Isaac was forty when he married, but neither his grief nor his mother's tent can be reasonably expected to have lasted for a quarter of a century.

1   *Ya-a*: On the sledge-shaped canopy (Cairo Museum Catalogue No. 51001), the mummy-shaped sarcophagus (51002), the mummy-shaped coffin of wood covered with silver leaf (51003) and a second mummy-shaped coffin covered with gold leaf (51004).

2   *Ya*: A variation on coffin No. 51004.

3   *Yi-Ya*: On bands which formed a cage around Yuya's mummy (51010) and three *ushabti* boxes (51041, 51043 and 51044).

4   *Yu-Ya*: On Yuya's canopic box (51012), eight *ushabti* (51025 and 51028–51034), an *ushabti* box (51041), two other boxes (51115 and 51116), a staff (51132) and a whipstock (51133).

5   *Ya-Yi*: On three *ushabti* (51024, 51026 and 51027).

6   *Yu*: On an *ushabti* box (51053).

7   *Yu-Yu*: On an *ushabti* box (51053) and the papyrus containing his copy of *The Book of the Dead* (51189) where his name is always spelled *Yu-Yu*.

8   *Ya-Ya*: On a model coffin (51054).

9   *Yi-Ay*: On two sets of four vases on stands (51102 and 51103).

10 *Yi-a*: On a limestone bird with a human face (51176).

11 *Yu-y*: On another canopic box (51012).

The name is written in all but two cases as two syllables—*Yu* on the lid of an *ushabti* box (although inside the same syllable is repeated as *Yu-Yu*) and *Ya* on a coffin. Every syllable begins with the letter 'Y', which in this case has to be read as a consonant because an Egyptian syllable cannot start with a vowel.

There are two important points about the relationship between Joseph's biblical name and the name of Yuya. In the first place, Joseph's biblical name, like Yuya's, is a composite one, Yu-seph—'Y' in Egyptian and Hebrew becomes 'J' in English, and, in both languages, 'o' and 'u' are written with the same sign—and the first syllable, which relates him to his God, *Yhwa* (Jehovah), is the same as the first syllable of Yuya's. Secondly, the variety in the spelling suggests that Yuya's name was a foreign one which the scribes found difficult to render into hieroglyphics.

Although he had Egyptian blood and had lived in Egypt for many years, Joseph was essentially a foreigner. There has also been speculation that Yuya, Amenhotep's father-in-law, might also have been a foreigner. When Yuya's tomb was discovered, considerable interest centred around whether it contained any evidence to support this theory. James Quibell, the British archaeologist who supervised the excavation, took the view: 'The only piece of evidence in its favour is the great variety in the spelling of the name. One may suppose at any rate that it was a rare name and difficult to render in hieroglyphics; it is possible that it was a foreign word.' Gaston Maspero also commented on the same point: 'The man's name assumes several forms of spelling, which differ somewhat from each other (and) are not all to be found on the same monument. It appears that each scribe or craftsman employed in the making of the funeral furniture . . . adopted his own rendering of the name for the objects that he decorated.'

But what name were the scribes actually trying to write? Egyptian names usually indicated the god under whom the person concerned was placed—Re-mos, Ptah-hotep, Tutankh-Amun and so on. The evidence suggests that, despite the years he spent in Egypt and the high office he held, Joseph remained aloof from Egyptian religious worship: most scholars believe that the sudden appearance of the name of the god Aten during the Eighteenth Dynasty is connected with Yuya although it was his grandson, Akhnaten, who later developed the worship of this god into a monotheistic belief. The first mention of Aten during the Eighteenth Dynasty occurs, in fact, on a scarab dating from the reign of Tuthmosis IV, who appointed Joseph to the post of vizier. His son, Amenhotep III, subsequently built a temple to Aten in Nubia and the barge in which he sailed on Queen Tiye's pleasure lake was named *Aten Gleams*. It seems therefore a reasonable assumption that, by the time Joseph died, Egyptians must have realised that he would not accept the protection of any Egyptian gods, only his own God, *Yhwh* (Jehovah) or *Yhwa* (the final *h* is read as an *a* in Hebrew), and what they were trying to write, following the Egyptian tradition, was the first part of the name of his God. A further cause of confusion for the scribes and craftsmen employed on Yuya's tomb may have arisen from the names of his forebears. Jacob, Joseph's father, is also said to have died in Egypt, where he was embalmed. His name must therefore have been known to the Egyptians, but, although again based on the divine name, it was pronounced Ya. Then in the case of Isaac it was pronounced Yi. It seems that, in the face of these differences, the Egyptian scribes used all three readings of *Yhwa*, with Yuya the most common and Yi-w the nearest to the complete form.

Generally speaking, ancient Egyptian—in this respect the same as Semitic languages—does not use vowels: the scribe is taught how to

read in the correct vowels. Nevertheless, some consonants are used as
long vowels. In the case of Yuya long vowels were used in every case
because, with foreign names, no one could be expected to know the
correct form of the reading. Nowadays Yuya is the generally accepted
spelling of the name, but, misled by the use of long vowels, Gaston
Maspero, followed by other early Egyptologists, read the name as
Iouiya. It is an interesting sidelight that this interpretation is very
similar to the way—Yaouai—the early Christian writers between
AD 150 and 450 wrote the divine name, while in Greek letters in
Hellenistic magical forms it was written Ieoa.[1]

YUYA'S ORIGIN

Grafton Elliot Smith, the British anatomist who examined Yuya's
mummy in 1905, devoted part of his subsequent report[2] to whether he
might be of foreign origin. After describing the method used by the
embalmer, he went on: 'His (Yuya's) face is relatively short and
elliptical, the total facial height being only 110mm whereas the
bizygomatic breadth'—the distance between the two bony arches on
either side of the skull—'is 125mm. His nose is prominent, aquiline
and high-bridged: at the same time the alae (lateral cartilages) are
wide, probably more so than in life, because the nostrils have been
dilated in the process of packing the nasal fossae with linen. The bridge
of the nose projects 2cm in front of the canthi (outer and inner corners
of the eyes where the lids meet). The lips appear to be somewhat full.
The jaw is moderately square. The moustache had not been shaven for
two or three days before death, for the upper lip, chin and submental
region are thickly studded with white hairs, 2 or 3mm in length. The
eyebrows and eyelashes are well-preserved, but, unlike the other hair,
they are of a dark brown colour. Unlike the ears of most Royal
mummies of the New Empire, Yuaa's were not pierced.' He then
turned to consider Yuya's origin: 'When we come to enquire into the
racial character of the body of Yuya, there is very little we can
definitely seize on as a clear indication of his origin and affinities. In
norma verticalis his cranium is distinctly ovoid, almost beloid, i.e. it is
not broad enough to permit us to state definitely that it is not Egyptian,

[1] Introduction to the *New English Bible*.
[2] Published in *Catalogue général des antiquités égyptiennes du Musée du Caire,
Tomb of Yuaa and Thuiu*, James E. Quibell.

although its shape is by no means a common one in the pure Egyptian. The forehead is somewhat low and receding: the cranium as a whole is depressed, but the occiput is moderately prominent. The form of the face (and especially the nose) is such as we find more commonly in Europe than in Egypt.'

On the subject of Yuya's possible nationality, Smith observed that, while his mummy 'has a distinctly alien appearance, one would not be justified in concluding that it is not Egyptian, for we do meet with similar proportions in the faces of many individuals supposed to be Egyptians. Moreover, even if we go so far as to admit—which I am not prepared to do—that this face and cranium conform to an alien (non-Egyptian) racial type, it must not be forgotten that at all times during the historical periods in Egypt the upper classes intermingled with foreigners from neighbouring countries, so that—and this is especially the case in the delta—alien types may be found among people who have been settled for many generations.' Smith's final conclusion was: 'It is clear from these considerations that it would be rash to offer a final opinion on the subject of Yuaa's nationality.'

Scholarly opinion has since been divided about whether or not Yuya was a foreigner. Gaston Maspero, in his book *The Struggle of the Nations*, said he was convinced that both he and Tuya were Egyptian. Henri Naville felt, however, that the evidence was strong enough to disagree with him sharply: 'M. Maspero considers man and wife as being natives. It seems to me quite certain about the wife, looking at her type of face. If, as has been supposed, there is a foreign element about one of them, it must be Iouiya, whose type is different from that of his wife. His very aquiline face might be Semitic; besides, the numerous transcriptions of his name seem to show that, for the Egyptians, it was a foreign sound which they reproduced in writing as they heard it, just as in our time two Egyptians will not spell alike a German, French or English name.'[1]

While we can see how Joseph could have been transcribed into Yuya, the transformation of his wife, Asenath, into Tuya and his son, Ephraim, into Aye can only be a matter of conjecture. It is a fact that it was common practice at the time for the Egyptians to have several names, some of which were kept secret. Tutankhamun, for instance, had five—the one by which he is commonly known and, in addition,

[1] *Funerary Papyrus of Iouiya.*

Ka-Nekhet Tutmes (his Horus name), Nefer-Hebo Gereḥ-Tawi (Nebti), Re-neb Ka-w Seḥetep Neteru (Golden Horus) and Neb Kheparu-Re (Nesubet). It was also the custom to use pet names as well as abbreviated forms for longer and more complex names. Some allowance must be made, too, for the fact that many centuries passed between the events described and the time they were set down in the Bible. To use a simple analogy, if the Tudor era were far more remote than it is and, as in the case of Egypt, vast quantities of the relevant documents had been destroyed, it might prove difficult to establish to everyone's satisfaction that Queen Elizabeth I and Queen Bess were the same person.

In relation to Asenath and Tuya, however, there is one striking piece of evidence. Scholars have explained that her name derives from the Egyptian *ns-nt*, which they have interpreted as meaning 'belonging to the goddess Neit'. This, as I mentioned earlier, is an arbitrary interpretation. Egyptian has no vowels: *ns-nt* could therefore be just as readily interpreted as 'belonging to the goddess Nut'. On Tuya's outer coffin she is addressed as *wrt ȝḫt*, which appears in the texts as an epithet—as the swastika is an epithet for Nazism—of the goddess Nut.

THE TWO VIZIERS

Although the name 'Seph' does not appear in any of the texts found in Yuya's tomb, Josephus informs us in his book *Contra Apionem* that Manetho, quoting ancient Egyptian tradition, gave the name of the leader of the Jews in Egypt during the reign of Amenophis (Amenhotep III), the eighth king in his list for the Eighteenth Dynasty, as Osarseph. Osar, the first part of this name, is a transliteration of the Egyptian *wsr*—Greek, the language used by Manetho, does not have a letter 'W'—which was the ancient Egyptian name for Osiris, king of the underworld, and was later used as a title, *wasir* (it is the Turkish version of this title, vizier, that has passed into English usage). We therefore have accounts of a vizier named Yu and another named Seph, both alive at the time of Amenhotep III.[1]

---

[1] Manetho, whose work was based on a long oral tradition with the inevitable distortions that occur when stories are handed down by word of mouth, wrongly identified 'vizier Seph' as the leader of the Exodus, which, again wrongly, he placed in the reign of Amenhotep III. It is interesting, however, that Egyptian tradition should point to this particular point in the Eighteenth Dynasty in Egypt as one of special significance in relation to the Israelites.

POSITIONS

The turning point in Joseph's life was his appointment as vizier to
Pharaoh when the functions and privileges conferred upon him are
given in the words of the king:

> Thou shalt be over my house, and according unto thy word shall
> all my people be ruled; only in the throne will I be greater than
> thou. *Genesis* 41:40.

Yahuda comments in his book *The Language of the Pentateuch in its
Relation to Egyptian* on the language used by the Hebrew narrator to
describe Joseph's position: 'For this office Genesis gives . . . *mshna*.
This expression is formed from *sh-n-a*, to do twice, to repeat, to
double, in the sense that he represented in relation to the king a sort of
"double" acting as the deputy, invested with all the rights and
prerogatives of the king. In the same way the Egyptian word *sn.nw*,
"deputy", was formed from *sn*, "two".' This corresponds exactly with
the evidence found in Yuya's tomb where he is given the same title:
'whom the king has made his double'.

In his book *Ancient Records of Egypt*, John H. Breasted gives an
account of the duties of a vizier, obtained from the tomb of Rakhmira,
who occupied that position during the reign of Tuthmosis III, the
period of Egypt's greatest power, around the time of Yuya's birth. The
duties he describes—apart from the fact that, significantly, there is no
mention of chariotry—are similar to those accorded to Joseph in the
Bible: 'It will be seen that the vizier is the grand steward of all Egypt,
and that all the activities of the state are under his control. He has
general oversight of the treasury and the chief treasurer reports to him;
he is chief justice or head of the justiciary; he is chief of police, both for
the residence city and kingdom; he is minister of war, both for army
and navy; he is secretary of the interior and of agriculture, while all
general executive functions of state, with many that may not be
classified, are incumbent upon him. There is, indeed, no prime func-
tion of state that does not operate through his office. He is a veritable
Joseph, and it must be this office which the Hebrew writer has in mind
in the story of Joseph.'

THE KING'S RING

When the king appointed Joseph, he gave him three objects as a sign of
his office:

And Pharaoh took off his ring from his hand, and put it upon Joseph's hand, and arrayed him in vestures of fine linen, and put a gold chain about his neck. *Genesis* 41:42.

There were two attempts to steal small objects from Yuya's tomb, one in ancient times, just after the burial, and the other after the tomb was opened in 1905. Quibell was able to buy back some of the stolen objects in Luxor market. The ring might have disappeared as a result of either of these robberies, but we do have written evidence of its existence in the tomb. Yuya, like many other viziers, was 'bearer of the seal of the king of Lower Egypt' as well as 'bearer of the ring of the king of Lower Egypt', which was translated by Naville as 'chancellor'.[1]

THE GOLD CHAIN

The honour bestowed upon Joseph by the presentation of a gold chain was mentioned in texts before the New Kingdom, but it is not until the reign of Tuthmosis IV, who appointed Joseph as his vizier, that the presentation becomes the subject for the artist. The best examples belong to the time of the Amarna kings, Yuya's descendants.

The receiving of gold was looked upon as one of the highest distinctions of the time, and, as we saw before, Yuya had a gold necklace that had fallen inside his coffin and come to rest under his head when the thread was cut by robbers.

THE CHARIOT

By making Joseph ride 'in his second chariot' Pharaoh was indicating his position as head of the chariotry. This responsibility is confirmed by two of the titles found in Yuya's tomb, Master of the Horse and Deputy of His Majesty in the Chariotry. In fact, according to the Haggadah (Sefer ha-Yashar, section Mikkez) Joseph is said to have equipped a considerable army with which he marched to help the Ishmaelites against the Tarshishites, winning a great victory.

It was the custom in ancient Egypt to place in a tomb objects that had had a special significance for the deceased during his life. The chariot found in Yuya's tomb is another indication of his position. The chariot is too small to be his own, yet too large to be a model. It is possible that the chariot belonged originally to Tuthmosis IV, a young

[1] *The Funerary Papyrus of Iouiya.*

The brick 'store chambers' discovered by Henri Naville at Tell el-Maskhuta which led him to believe he had found one of the biblical store cities of the Exodus story. *Photo: Cairo Museum*

Seti I with his son Prince Ramses make an offering before the cartouches of the royal ancestors. From the Temple of Abydos. *Photo: Cairo Museum*

Asiatic and negro prisoners from the tomb of Horemheb, illustrating his career as commander-in-chief and regent of Tutankhamun, before he became King of Egypt. From Sakkara. *Photo: Cairo Museum*

Horemheb as a scribe, before he seized the throne. The statue on the left was found at Memphis, that on the right at Karnak. *Photos: left, All rights reserved, The Metropolitan Museum of Art, New York; right, Cairo Museum*

Aye, thought to be Yuya's son, and his wife Tey receiving rewards from Akhnaten. Found at Amarna. *Photo: Cairo Museum*

Anen, brother of Queen Tiye and Yuya's elder son, Priest of On (Heliopolis), Second Prophet of Amun. *Photo: Museo Egizio, Turin*

Yuya, with his wife standing behind him, faces Osiris. His white wig shows him to be an old man. The text reads: 'Adoring Osiris, kissing the ground before Unefris. Said by the divine father of the Lord of the Two Lands, The favoured of the good god, Yuya . . .' From *The Book of the Dead in Yuya's*

Amenhotep, son of Habu, a magician of Yuya's time said to have lived 110 years. This dark granite statue, found at Karnak, shows him at the age of 80. *Photos: Cairo Museum*

One of the sandstone Osirian pillar statues of Amenhotep IV (Akhnaten) from the Aten temple at Karnak. *Photo: Cairo Museum*

Stele representing Akhnaten, his wife Nefertiti and three of their daughters. Akhnaten is holding out an earring to the eldest, Merytaten, while Meketaten stands on the edge of her mother's chair and Ankhsenpaaten, later to be married to Tutankhamun, sits on Nefertiti's lap. Limestone, found in a shrine of a private house at Tell el-Amarna. *Photo: Cairo Museum*

Upper part of an altar in the form of a gateway decorated with reliefs of Akhnaten, Nefertiti and their daughter Merytaten, offering to Aten. Limestone, from a private house at Tell el-Amarna. *Photo: Cairo Museum*

a. Head of Tutankhamun from a coronation group in which the god Amun is placing his hand on the head-dress of Tutankhamun. *Photo: All rights reserved, The Metropolitan Museum of Art, New York.* b. Tutankhamun between the god Amun and the goddess Nut. *Photo: Cairo Museum*

A 'dummy' of Tutankhamun, made of stuccoed and painted wood. From his tomb. *Photo: Cairo Museum*

boy when he appointed Joseph, and could have been one that he used when he was crown prince. This would explain why, although ornamented in gold, it was not inscribed.

THE KING'S CATTLE

When his brothers came to settle in Egypt, Joseph presented five of them to the king, who said:

> . . . The best of the land of Egypt is before thee; in the best of the land make thy father and brethren to dwell; in the land of Goshen let them dwell: and if thou knowest any men of activity among them, then make them rulers over my cattle. *Genesis* 47:6.

Two of the titles found in Yuya's tomb were Overseer of the Cattle of Min, Lord of Akhmin, and Overseer of the Cattle of Amun.

JOSEPH'S WIFE

In addition to being made vizier, Joseph was given an Egyptian wife by Pharaoh, 'the daughter of the priest of On'. Tuya's tomb gives no indication of who her father was, but the fact that she was connected, through being Mistress of the Harem in both places, with the temples of Amun at Thebes and Min at Akhmin, indicates that she came from a priestly background.

More significant in this respect is the priestly position held by her son Anen, whose name appears twice on her outer coffin: 'her son, the second prophet of Amun, praised of the good god, Anen'. An inscribed statue of Anen, now in Turin, identifies him also as the priest of On (Heliopolis). If this position was hereditary, as was the case with the Memphite priests, it is possible that Anen could have inherited his position as priest of On from his maternal grandfather, Tuya's father.[1]

THE TWO PHARAOHS

Yuya served two Pharaohs—Tuthmosis IV and his son, Amenhotep III. Similarly, the Talmud indicates that the Pharaoh who appointed Joseph died before him and Joseph served the following king, his son:

---

[1] A list of kings from the Eleventh Dynasty to the time of Shoshenk of the Twenty-second Dynasty, with the names of Memphis priests—all claiming to belong to one family—serving under every king, is described in *Egypt of the Pharaohs* by Alan Gardiner.

'And it came to pass . . . that Pharaoh the friend of Joseph died . . . Before his death Pharaoh commanded his son, who succeeded him, to obey Joseph in all things, and the same instructions he left in writing. This pleased the people of Egypt, for they loved Joseph and trusted implicitly in him. Thus while this Pharaoh reigned over Egypt the country was governed by Joseph's advice and counsel.'[1]

CHILDREN

The Bible states that Joseph's Egyptian wife bore him two sons, Manasseh and Ephraim. No mention is made of a daughter. This is not unusual, however. The Bible does not usually refer to female descendants unless it is relevant to the story being told. Therefore the absence of any mention of a daughter cannot be taken as proof that Joseph did not have one: otherwise we should be forced to the conclusion that, apart from the few women who are mentioned, the Hebrews fathered only male descendants.

The Bible gives us an indirect indication that Joseph had a daughter. When Jacob died and Joseph wanted to bury him in Canaan, he had first to obtain the king's permission. Yet, although Joseph was the vizier and the closest official to Pharaoh, he did not ask the king himself, but instead used the services of a mediator. Normally the mediator is someone who is closer to both sides than they are to each other. Whom did Joseph choose?

> And when the days of his mourning were past, Joseph spake unto the house of Pharaoh, saying, If now I have found grace in your eyes, speak, I pray you, in the ears of Pharaoh . . . *Genesis* 50:4.

The expression 'the house of Pharaoh' in ancient Egypt meant his wife, the queen. The expression is still used today: it is not considered polite to speak directly about a person's wife or mention her name, and, even if she has no children, a wife would still be referred to as 'the house' of her husband. An example of this we have already seen in the biography of Ahmose, son of Abana, recorded on the walls of his tomb: 'I took service in his (his father's) stead, in the ship of *The Wild Bull*, in the

[1] *Selections from the Talmud*, translated from the original by H. Polano. The omissions are that Joseph's death occurred in the thirty-second year after the arrival of the Israelites and that he was aged seventy-one at the time. However, the Talmud is even more suspect than the Old Testament in anything pertaining to dates, ages or figures.

time of the Lord of the Two Lands, the justified Nebpehti-re (Ahmosis I), when I was a youth and had not taken a wife, but spent my nights in a hammock of net. Now, when I had established a house (married), I was taken upon the ship *Northern* because I was valiant . . .'

The same expression is used at the beginning of the account of how Joseph eventually revealed himself to his brothers when they made their second trip to Egypt to buy corn:

And he (Joseph) wept aloud: and the Egyptians and the house of Pharaoh heard. *Genesis* 45:2.

In this second case the verse can be interpreted as either meaning that Joseph's house was so near to Pharaoh's that the queen heard his weeping or that the news about Joseph's brothers was sent to the queen because she would be interested. In the first, however, while we can understand how the queen would be nearer to the king than his vizier was, in what circumstances could she also be nearer to Joseph than Pharaoh was? There can be no satisfactory explanation for this situation unless Queen Tiye was the daughter of both Yuya and Joseph.

In this connection it is interesting that there is a missing person in the various references in Genesis to the number of Israelites who made the Descent into Egypt. All the souls of the house of Jacob who came into Egypt, including Joseph and his sons, are described as totalling seventy in number (*Genesis* 46:27). However, the number of Jacob's descendants from Leah are given as thirty-three, of whom two died in Canaan before the Descent, leaving thirty-one (*Genesis* 46:15), the number of Jacob's descendants from Zilpah as sixteen (*Genesis* 46:18), the number of Jacob's descendants from Rachel, including Joseph and his two sons, as fourteen (*Genesis* 46:22), and the number from Bilhah as seven (*Genesis* 46:25). If we add Jacob himself to the list, we are still left with a total of only sixty-nine, not seventy. Similarly, there is another reference to the number of Jacob's descendants who went down to Egypt as sixty-six (*Genesis* 46:26), indicating that four were already in Egypt: yet we are given the names of only three. On the basis of the biblical figures, and those of the second reference in particular, it is a reasonable assumption that the seventieth person was also already in Egypt—Joseph's daughter. It is possible that, if she had married into the Egyptian Royal family, once friends and later oppressors, her name was a deliberate omission by the Hebrew scribes when they edited the Bible story.

As for the two sons, we know from an inscription on Tuya's sarcophagus that she had a son named Anen, who was the second prophet of Amun. There is no mention of another son, but the argument has been strong in favour of there having been one, Aye. Alan Gardiner commented in *Egypt of the Pharaohs*: 'Yuya in his tomb at Thebes bore the title Overseer of Horses, while Aye at el-Amarna is Overseer of all the Horses of His Majesty. Even more remarkable is the connection of both with the town of Akhmin, where Yuya was a prophet of Min as well as superintendent of that god's cattle, and where King Aye erected a shrine and left a long inscription. Just as Yuya's wife Tuya was the mother of Queen Tiye, the spouse of King Aye had previously been the nurse of Queen Nefertiti. Little wonder if, in view of these facts, Percy E. Newberry proposed that Yuya and Aye, as well as their wives Tuya and Tey, were actually one and the same. It must be understood that the names which, in a purely conventional manner, we render in different ways, offer no real obstacle to this theory: such is the nature of hieroglyphic writing at this period that we cannot be sure that what appears to be written as Yuya may not have been pronounced Aye, and similarly with the names of the wives. Chronologically, however, Newberry's view, which he himself never published, is absolutely impossible: since, moreover, the mummies of both Yuya and Tuya, evidently very aged people, were discovered in their Theban tomb, it would be necessary to assume that Yuya or Aye, whichever pronunciation we might prefer for him, had before his death been forced to renounce his kingly title and to revert to the position of a commoner. Cyril Aldred has made the plausible suggestion that the future monarch Aye was the son of Yuya: this certainly would explain the similarity of their titles and their close connection with Akhmin. The author also noted a striking resemblance between Yuya's mummy and a portrait of Aye as king, depicted as the Nile God, at the base of a statue now in the Museum of Fine Arts in Boston.'

If, as is now generally thought, Yuya, like Joseph, had two sons, and it was the younger one who reached the higher position when he became king of Egypt after Tutankhamun's death, this would explain—which the Bible itself does not do—the biblical story of Jacob's blessing for Joseph's younger son.

THE AGE OF WISDOM

Genesis tell us that Joseph died 'being an hundred and ten years old' (Gen. 50:26). Ancient Egyptians considered old age to be a sign of wisdom and those who attained long life were looked upon as being holy figures. In our case, both Joseph and Yuya were considered wise by Pharaoh. Of Joseph, he said: '. . . there is none so discreet and wise as thou art' (*Genesis* 41:39). Yuya is also described on his funerary papyrus as 'the only wise, who loves his god'.[1] The age the Egyptians gave to those who lived to be wise was one hundred and ten years, irrespective of their real age when they died. Amenhotep son of Habu, an Egyptian magician in Yuya's time, was said to have lived one hundred and ten years although the last information we have of him puts his age at eighty. Since 1865, when Charles W. Goodwin suggested that the age the biblical narrator assigned to Joseph at the time of his death was a reflection of the Egyptian tradition, this idea has become more and more accepted by Egyptologists and was further reinforced when Gustave Lefebvre and Josef M. Janssen were able to show from Egyptian texts that at least twenty-seven characters were said to have reached the age of one hundred and ten years.

From the medical report made by Grafton Elliot Smith, we know that Yuya probably was not less than sixty at his death. Smith was unable, judging by facial appearance alone, to decide the exact age, but Henri Naville, who translated Yuya's copy of *The Book of the Dead*, wrote in his subsequent commentary upon it: 'In both cases the artist wished to indicate clearly that Iouiya was a very old man when he died: therefore he made him quite a white wig . . .'

Both Joseph and Yuya therefore died at a very old age, the age of wisdom for the Egyptians, one hundred and ten years.

JOSEPH'S BURIAL

The last verse of the Book of Genesis describes the final rites of Joseph:

So Joseph died, being an hundred and ten years old: and they embalmed him, and he was put in a coffin in Egypt. *Genesis* 50:26.

But, because of the two preceding verses, the story of Joseph does not end there:

[1] *The Funerary Papyrus of Iouiya*, Henri Naville.

And Joseph said unto his brethren, I die: and God will surely visit
you, and bring you out of this land unto the land which he sware
to Abraham, to Isaac, and to Jacob. And Joseph took an oath of
the children of Israel, saying, God will surely visit you, and ye
shall carry up my bones from hence. *Genesis* 50:24, 25.

This is a complete change in Joseph's attitude to settling in Egypt. He
arrived in the country, according to the Bible, at the age of seventeen
and was appointed vizier, the most powerful post in the country after
that of Pharaoh, when he was thirty. He made no attempt to contact
his family and it was only when his brothers came to Egypt to buy corn
that he was eventually reunited with them. In addition, by accepting an
Egyptian woman as his wife he knew that his children would be
brought up as Egyptians, for it was the Israelite custom that the
children followed their mother, not their father. Even when his father,
Jacob, died and Joseph went up to Canaan with all his brothers to bury
him, he still came back, as did all the Israelites, to live in Egypt, their
new home. Why, then, should he change his mind suddenly at the time
of his death? Or did he? When Jacob felt that his end was near, he
asked Joseph to 'bury me with my fathers' and his wish was carried
out. Why did not Joseph do the same if he wished to be buried in
Canaan? Furthermore, if he foresaw trouble for the Israelites in the
future should they continue to live in Egypt, why did he not advise
them not only to take his body back to his homeland but themselves
leave forthwith? Otherwise, of what value was his prophecy? He took
practical steps to deal with the famine he foretold from Pharaoh's
dreams: why did he not do the same here?[1]

Then again, as Egyptians used to place some valuable objects in their
tombs, they took the precaution of keeping the whereabouts of the
tomb a secret. We are even told that in some cases kings buried the
architect who had planned their tomb inside it so as to keep the
entrances completely unknown. In the face of such customs, how
would the fourth generation of Israelites have known where to find the
tomb of Joseph?

Donald B. Redford believes that the verses reporting Joseph's death
were not included in the original story, but are the work of a later

---

[1] A contradictory chronology for these events comes from rabbinical sources to the
effect that it was the second generation of the Israelites who, after Joseph's death, went
up to Canaan to bury Jacob's other sons, leaving Joseph still buried in Egypt.

editor. How did this come about? Redford explains in *A Study of the Biblical Story of Joseph*: 'With the pattern of Jacob's death and burial before him, the Genesis editor could have made the family trek a second time to Palestine to bury Joseph. This would have been the most reasonable procedure. But he did not choose such an expedient. Instead, he adopted the most unlikely course of having Joseph's body kept in a coffin in Egypt for five hundred-odd years until, after the Israelite Exodus and Conquest, it was finally buried at Shechem. Why? Because the Genesis editor had no authorisation in his sources to do otherwise . . . the Joseph story told of only one trip to Palestine with the purpose of burying Jacob: another source, the Exodus tradition, told of a second trip, viz. the Exodus. Between these two egressions from Egypt, the Genesis editor had no evidence for another, and could not invent one.'

In order to reinforce the implications of the two verses mentioned above, the biblical editor introduced two later verses, one in the Book of Exodus, the second in Joshua:

> And Moses took the bones of Joseph with him: for he had straitly sworn the children of Israel, saying, God will surely visit you; and ye shall carry up my bones away hence with you. *Exodus* 13:19.

> And the bones of Joseph, which the children of Israel brought up out of Egypt, buried they in Shechem, in a parcel of ground which Jacob bought of the sons of Hamor, the father of Shechem . . . *Joshua* 24:32.

Two points need to be made before examining the original Hebrew texts relating to the removal of Joseph's bones. The first is the use of the word 'bones' for Joseph's mummy. It is obvious that the scribe who edited the story had no idea of how an embalmed body would look: Yuya, after thirty-three centuries, looked as if he had just died a few days ago. The second point concerns the position of the intruding verse in the Book of Joshua. It comes not as soon as the Israelites arrive in Canaan, but at the very end (Josh. 24:32), three verses after Joshua has been reported dead (Josh. 24:29). This suggests that it was not part of the original story, and such a view is reinforced by the original Hebrew text. The divine name is not mentioned in the Joshua reference to the bones of Joseph, but it occurs nineteen times in Chapter 13 of Exodus. In fifteen cases it is given as Jehovah and in four—all relating to the

Exodus and the removal of Joseph's bones—as Elohim. This again indicates a later insertion.

It would seem that the later editors did not like the idea that the Patriarch was still buried in the land of the oppressors when the Exodus had become the cornerstone in the new religion of the Jews. How else would it be possible to understand how Moses, the greatest Israelite leader, who supposedly carried Joseph's bones with him to Sinai, was himself left buried in an unmarked grave when he died?

> So Moses the servant of the Lord died there in the land of Moab, according to the word of the Lord. And he (Joshua) buried him in a valley in the land of Moab, over against Beth-pe-or: but no man knoweth of his sepulchre unto this day. *Deuteronomy* 34:5, 6.

Chapter 13

DEATH OF THE GODS

The rule of Yuya's descendants—the Amarna kings, Amenhotep IV (Akhnaten), Semenkhkare, Tutankhamun and, lastly, Aye, who is generally regarded as Yuya's own son—saw one of the most extraordinary episodes in Egyptian history and was followed by another after the Amarna Age had ended. Firstly, Amenhotep IV closed down the temples and attempted to destroy the traditional gods of Egypt, replacing them with a monotheistic god, Aten, and changing his own name from Amenhotep IV to Akhnaten: then, after Horemheb, the last king of the Eighteenth Dynasty, had replaced the Amarna kings, a concerted attempt was made to wipe their names out of Egyptian history as if they had never existed.

The gods of Egypt were many and varied, some deities of purely local significance, others, like Seth, Re and Osiris, accepted throughout the country. As we saw earlier, Aten was not a newcomer to the scene. However, although his name does appear in a few texts from the time of the Twelfth Dynasty, it reappears consistently from the time of Tuthmosis IV when he is first mentioned on a scarab. Amenhotep III, the son of Tuthmosis IV, later built a temple to Aten in Nubia and also had a barge named *Aten Gleams* in which he sailed on the pleasure lake he constructed for Queen Tiye. Akhnaten singled this god out from the others. Unlike them, he had no anthropomorphic representation, no image, but was represented simply by a sun disc in the same way as the Cross is today the symbol of Christianity.

This major change began about the fourth year of Akhnaten's reign when a large temple to Aten was erected to the east of the great temple to Amun at Karnak. Amun had been concealed in a dark shrine at Karnak: Aten was worshipped in a sanctuary that had no roof. The temple walls bore brightly painted scenes depicting the jubilee that the king had celebrated with Aten, whose eminence was indicated by the fact that his names, like those of kings, were written in cartouches. At about the time that he changed his name to conform to his new monotheistic religion, Akhnaten abandoned Thebes as his capital in favour of a new one—Akhetaten, the city of the horizon—which he built at Tell el-Amarna in Middle Egypt, halfway between Memphis and Thebes. The new city was planned thoughtfully, with temples to Aten, palaces, official buildings, villas for courtiers and quarters for labourers, tombs for high officials and a Royal sepulchre. Akhnaten's insistence on one God intensified with the passage of time until, after reigning for seventeen years, he disappeared mysteriously, having ruled jointly with Semenkhkare for the last three years. The latter also disappeared from the scene in an equally strange manner. Then came Tutankhamun, who is thought to be Akhnaten's son by his queen, Nefertiti, although some scholars believe he was yet a third son of Amenhotep III. Tutankhamun attempted a compromise between the Aten beliefs and the old gods. He left Amarna, returned to Thebes and reopened the closed temples, although he still allowed Aten to be worshipped in the city of the horizon.

The religious upheaval of these eventful years is described in the Restoration Stele which Tutankhamun erected after coming to the throne: '. . . the temples of the gods and goddesses from Elephantine to the marshes of the delta had gone to pieces, the shrines were desolate and overgrown with weeds . . . and the gods turned their backs upon this land.' The stele also records that the young king resorted to lavish gifts to try to win back the allegiance of the priests of Amun: '. . . he has increased their property in gold, silver, bronze and copper without limit, he has filled their workshops with male and female slaves . . . All the property of the temples has been doubled, tripled, quadrupled in silver, gold, lapis lazuli, turquoise . . . without limit to any good thing.' This generosity achieved only partial success for, after nine years, Tutankhamun met a violent end and was replaced by someone who appeared to have no legitimate claim to the throne—Yuya's younger son, Aye, who had served as vizier to Akhnaten, Semenkhkare and Tutankhamun. He seems to have strengthened his position by marrying Tutankhamun's widow, Ankhsenpaaten, but even so, he, too, lasted only a short time—four years—before disappearing without trace.

His successor was Horemheb, a general in the Egyptian Army, who has been described as 'a kind of General Franco' of his day and secured his seat on the throne by marrying Queen Nefertiti's sister,

Mutnedjemet. Horemheb concentrated on restoring the stability of the country by reforming the judicial system and laying down strict punishments for misdemeanours. He dismantled many of the monuments that Akhnaten had erected and replaced many of the cartouches of Tutankhamun with his own. Horemheb, who ruled for the better part of thirty years, had no son and therefore secured the succession for Ramses, the mayor of Zaru and the king's vizier, after his own death.

After the death of Aye, a heavy curtain fell over the fate of the four Amarna kings and their families. The name of Akhnaten, who was referred to as 'the scoundrel of Akhetaten (Amarna)', was not allowed to be mentioned in the Two Lands of Egypt. The Amarna kings were regarded as usurpers of the throne and their names were omitted, for example, from the ancestral king-lists of Seti I at Abydos as well as Sakkara. All Egyptian records ignored them, giving the name of Horemheb as the king who followed Amenhotep to the throne and leaving out Akhnaten, Semenkhkare, Tutankhamun and Aye altogether. The silence lasted more than three thousand years until at last, early in the last century, Egyptologists came across the strange figure of Akhnaten, carved on the walls of the Amarna rock tombs. Then, between 1883 and 1893, came the French mission to clear the tombs and make copies of the texts and reliefs on their walls, as well as those found on boundary stelae surrounding the city. The site did not become a focus of interest, however, until the discovery in 1887 of the Amarna Tablets—copies and originals of letters, written in Babylonian cuneiform, that were despatches between Amenhotep III and his son Akhnaten on the one hand and the rulers of Western Asia on the other. From these letters we now know the kind of relations that existed between the kings and vassals of Western Asia and the Egyptian court, as well as possessing valuable philological and geographical information about Syria-Palestine at a time just before the return of the Israelites from Egypt to Canaan.

Given the complexity of Egyptian religious ideas and the long time they took to develop, where lie the roots of upheaval in belief during Akhnaten's reign, the worship of one God who had no image? It is generally thought to have its origins with Yuya. Yet where would Yuya acquire these revolutionary ideas, so far removed from the centuries-old religious beliefs of Egypt—unless he were Joseph, himself a believer in a monotheistic God?

Thus my research had led me to believe that both historical Yuya and biblical Joseph are but one and the same person, when I finally flew to Cairo in 1984 to see the man's mummy for myself.

The ground floor hall of Cairo Museum is dominated by a statue of Queen Tiye, Yuya's daughter, sitting next to her husband, Amenhotep III, in a huge composition that is seven metres high and five metres wide. The queen, for the first time in ancient Egyptian history, is shown as the same size as the king. Four years earlier, President Anwar al-Sadat had ordered the museum's mummy hall to be closed because he did not think it fitting that idle visitors should stare at the dead. Fortunately, as Yuya was not looked upon as a Royal personage, his remains were not kept in the mummy hall, but on the first floor where, to my disappointment, I discovered that the mummy was hidden out of sight inside an inner coffin.

I went to the office of Dr Mahammad Saleh, the museum's director, and explained that I was engaged in some research involving the tomb of Yuya and would like to take some pictures. Dr Saleh said helpfully that he would ask the museum's photographer to take the shots I wanted provided that I paid for them, but he refused to have the coffin opened. For that, he said, I would have to apply to the director-general of the antiquities department, giving my reasons. I realised that this might involve several days' delay and that my reasons for wanting to see the mummy might not convince the authorities. It therefore seemed sensible to do what I already had permission to do. With a hastily summoned crew, including a photographer, light operators and guards, one of the museum's officials and I made our way to the Yuya section, which was closed to the general public. Here the photographer took several shots of the coffin and the funerary furniture from various angles. As the work progressed, I took the museum official to one side and told him I would be grateful for a glimpse of the mummy inside its coffin. He said the rules forbade it. Nevertheless, he quietly singled out a key from a large bunch he carried and opened the glass frame within which the coffin was laid. The lid of the coffin was raised and I looked in.

I saw a long, thin face, dignified, almost alive, wearing a calm and confident expression. One could imagine that its owner had died only a day or two earlier. What attracted my attention most was the position of the mummy's hands. They are normally crossed over the chest in the Osirian position: here, the only example I have ever seen, the palms of both hands were placed face down on the chest, just under the chin, as if giving reverence, not to the gods but to himself. After twenty years of research, I felt I was looking on the face of patriarch Joseph of the Bible and the Koran, that I knew him.

Later, I was interviewed by Cairo's *October* magazine. It was then, for the first time, that I voiced the view that the mummy known as Yuya was actually that of Joseph. Nevertheless, Dr Saleh completely rejected the notion and subsequently discussed the matter with Thomas James, Keeper of Egyptian Antiquities at the British Museum and, at the time of writing, the chairman of the Egypt Exploration Society in London. Mr James agreed with Dr Saleh's view. I had already.returned to London when I heard of this discussion and I made an appointment with Mr James, who had kindly agreed to see me. I asked if it was not true that Yuya bore the title 'father to Pharaoh'? Mr James, like Dr Saleh, took the view that Yuya's title was only the semi-priestly one, 'father of the god', which was a common title in ancient Egypt. At this point I produced a photocopy of Yuya's titles, taken from the book written in 1907 by Theodore M. Davis, and pointed out that one of them was *it ntr n nb tawi*, the holy father of the Lord of the Two Lands, and not just the common semi-priestly *it ntr*, the father of the god. Mr James left his office and returned five minutes later with a copy of Davis's book, opened at the page listing Yuya's titles. Still looking at the inscription, he said: 'It is a matter that needs further consideration. I admit it is an additional point. If we are going to get nearer to the truth, this is a good reason for re-examination.'

That is what I have attempted in these pages. I hope it will inspire a new examination of Yuya's mummy, using modern scientific methods, and, if such an examination confirms my thesis, that the ultimate outcome may be a realisation of an old dream of President Sadat's— that one day a shrine will be built on the holy ground of Mount Sinai where Jews, Christians and Muslims can pray together in peace. Nobody has a greater claim to be the centrepiece of such a shrine than Joseph, who is revered by the followers of all three religions.

We are all the creatures of our childhood experiences: in the same way, I believe, nations can be the victims of their past. The Exodus was a profound and damaging experience for both Israelites and Egyptians, giving rise to a mysterious enmity, with neither side able to forgive the other. Although insults and oppressions were constantly remembered, all traces of blood relations between the two nations were destroyed. In Egypt, the names of the four kings who had Israelite blood were banned, while the biblical editors tried to cover up any memory of such a link, even to the extent of suggesting, to make the Exodus a complete separation, that the bones of Joseph had been removed at that time for re-burial in Canaan.

After the Amarna religious revolution and the Jewish Exodus, Egypt never really went back to the worship of its old gods. Instead, from the time of the Nineteenth Dynasty a new form of the worship of Osiris, who was assassinated by his brother Seth, developed and became the popular religion in Egypt, preparing the way for Christianity to take over, with the result that Egypt became the first Christian nation in the world in the first century AD. Then a complete acceptance of the God of Moses took place with the arrival of Islam in the seventh century AD.

Politically, too, the traumas of the Amarna period and the Exodus seem to have had their effect. Not long after the departure of the Israelites, Egypt fell under foreign rule, a domination that lasted in one form or another from the eleventh century BC until as recently as 1952, when Egyptian officers took over power from Farouk, the king of Albanian origin. It almost coincided with the Israeli homecoming.

The Jews, for their part, wandered the earth for centuries, feeling, wherever they went, like strangers whose souls could not rest until a link had been re-established with Zion, their spiritual fountain: if a Jew can belong to Zion, he will be fulfilled. A new Messianic age began with the founding of Israel in 1948. Today the whole of the land of Palestine is under Israeli control. On the map we find a Mount Zion in Jerusalem, on which the church of Mary, the mother of Jesus, was built, but no city of Zion, the central focus of Israelite dream and worship, has so far been identified. Where is it?

But that, and the true identity of Moses, is another story.

Book Two

NOTES AND SOURCES

Chapter 1

ABRAHAM'S VICTIM

The conclusions I have arrived at regarding the relationship between Abraham (Ibrahim) and Isaac (Ishak) from the evidence of the biblical narrations are in complete contrast to what I was brought up to believe as a Muslim. We were taught that, contrary to what the Bible states, it was Ishmael (Ismael), his son from Hagar, and not Isaac, who was the intended subject of Abraham's sacrifice. Thus, my interpretation of the sacrifice of Isaac as implying that Abraham, by his action, was trying to be rid of the fruit of a sinful marriage between Pharaoh and Sarah would not be possible if the victim was actually Ishmael.

In accepting that Isaac was the sacrificial victim, I found myself totally opposed to the views of modern Muslim scholars. However, on re-examination of the story of the sacrifice in the Koran, it becomes clear that the name of Abraham's intended victim is never stated directly. The account given in Sura XXXVII: 101–113 of the Koran follows immediately after a narration—which does not appear in the Bible, but is found in the Talmud—of a conflict between Abraham and his father, who worshipped idols. As a consequence, Abraham is thrown on a burning fire, but God saves him and Abraham decides to leave his father's house and land. The Koran story goes on:

> (101) So We gave him
> The good news
> Of a boy ready
> To suffer and forbear:
>
> (102) Then, when (the son)
> Reached (the age of)
> (Serious) work with him,
> He said: 'O my son!
> I see in vision
> That I offer thee in sacrifice:

(113)   We blessed him and Isaac:
         But of their progeny
         Are (some) that do right,
         And (some) that obviously
         Do wrong, to their own souls.

The sequence of this account is what has persuaded Islamic scholars to conclude that Ishmael was the object of the intended sacrifice, in spite of the Koran's failure to mention his name in this context. Firstly, we have the decision of Abraham to leave home after the quarrel with his father; then the announcement of a son to be born, not giving any name, although we know that Ishmael was Abraham's first-born (v. 101); then the intended sacrifice (v. 103), and finally the mention of Isaac (v. 112).

Although the view of Muslim theologians might sound logical, the Koran itself does not seem to have followed the same logic. The account given in Sura XXXVII of Abraham's conflict with his father, their subsequent separation and God's announcement to him of a son finds a place in four other chapters of the Koran. After giving the above story, Sura VI says:

(84)   We gave him Isaac
         And Jacob: all (three)
         We guided:
         And before him,
         We guided Noah,
         And among his progeny,
         David, Solomon, Job,
         Joseph, Moses and Aaron:
         Thus do We reward
         Those who do good.

There is no mention here of Ishmael although his name appears very shortly afterwards (v. 86) as one of Abraham's descendants. We come then to Sura XIX, which has the following verse after the story:

(49)   When he had turned away
         From them and from those
         Whom they worshipped besides
         Allah, We bestowed on him
         Isaac and Jacob, and each one
         Of them We made a prophet.

Once again Ishmael is not mentioned in this narration. The same is true of the account in Sura XXI:

> (72)   And we bestowed on him Isaac
>   And, as an additional gift,
>   (A grandson), Jacob, and We
>   Made righteous men of every one
>   (Of them).

And yet again in Sura XXIX:

> (27)   And We gave (Abraham)
>   Isaac and Jacob, and ordained
>   Among his progeny Prophethood
>   And Revelation, and We
>   Granted him his reward
>   In this life; and he was
>   In the Hereafter (of the company)
>   Of the Righteous.

In all of these cases, when the logic of Muslim theologians would make us expect the name of Ishmael, his first-born, to follow the departure of Abraham from his father's house and land, he is not mentioned at all. Instead, it is the name of Isaac that appears, followed by that of his own second son, Jacob. The Koran, which does not mention the name of Esau, the first-born of Isaac's twin sons, seems to have decided from the very outset that Jacob was his father's rightful heir. How then can we be expected to believe that only in the account of the intended sacrifice in Sura XXXVII, where no specific name is mentioned, that Ishmael's name is implied?

There is other conclusive evidence that the announcement in Sura XXXVII (v. 101) could not refer to anyone but Isaac. The Arabic involved comes from a verb, *bash-shara*, which means 'to relate or announce good news' and often occurs in connection with the birth of a child. In the Koran, however, we find this verb used to indicate the birth of only three boys: John the Baptist, Jesus and Isaac. The first case, which appears in Sura III and is repeated in Sura XIX, concerns the 'announcement' made to Zacharias:

> (38)   There did Zakariya
>   Pray to his Lord, saying:
>   'O my Lord! Grant unto me

From thee a progeny
That is pure; for Thou
Art He that heareth prayer!'

(39)   While he was standing
In prayer in the chamber,
The angels called unto him:
'Allah doth give thee
Glad tidings of Yahya (John the Baptist),
Witnessing the truth
Of a word from Allah, and (be
Besides) noble, chaste,
And a Prophet—
Of the (goodly) company
Of the righteous.'

(40)   He said: 'O my Lord!
How shall I have a son,
Seeing I am very old,
And my wife is barren?'
'Thus,' was the answer,
'Doth Allah accomplish
What he willeth.'

The second case, a few verses later in Sura III, speaks of an 'announcement' to Mary, the mother of Jesus:

(45)   Behold! the angels said:
'O Mary! Allah giveth thee
Glad tidings of a Word
From Him: his name
Will be Christ Jesus,
The son of Mary, held in honour
In this world and the Hereafter
And of (the company of) those
Nearest to Allah.

(46)   'He shall speak to the people
In childhood and in maturity,
And he shall be (of the company)
Of the righteous.'

(47)   She said: 'O my Lord!
How shall I have a son
When no man hath touched me?'
He said: 'Even so:
Allah createth
What He willeth:
When He hath decreed
A plan, He but saith
To it, "Be," and it is . . .'

In the third case, in Sura XI, we have an account virtually the same as
that of the biblical visitations which promised Abraham that Sarah
would bear him a son:

(69)   There came Our Messengers
To Abraham with glad tidings.
They said, 'Peace!' He answered,
'Peace!' and hastened
To entertain them
With a roasted calf.

(70)   But when he saw
Their hands went not
Towards the (meal), he felt
Some mistrust of them.
They said: 'Fear not:
We have been sent
Against the people of Lot.'

(71)   And his wife was standing
(There) and she laughed;
But We gave her
Glad tidings of Isaac,
And after him of Jacob.

(72)   She said: 'Alas for me!
Shall I bear a child,
Seeing I am an old woman,
And my husband here
Is an old man?
That would indeed
Be a wonderful thing.'

(73)   They said: 'Dost thou
        wonder at Allah's decree?
        The grace of Allah
        And his blessings on you.
        O ye people of the house!
        For He is indeed
        Worthy of all praise,
        Full of all glory!'

There are other references to this same story. It appears, with fewer
details, in Sura XV, in which Isaac's name is not mentioned, but is
indicated by the word 'boy' (v. 53); again in Sura XXIX, which
contains a synopsis of the story (v. 31), and yet again in Sura LI, which
gives the story in full but refers only to a 'boy'. In each case, whether or
not Isaac is named specifically, there is no argument about the fact that
he is the person indicated.

As we can see, on the only three occasions in the Koran in which
God announced a forthcoming birth to a child's parent or parents, a
miraculous element was involved: Mary was a virgin and, in the cases
of Zacharias and Abraham, both were advanced in years and their
wives were considered to be barren. This indicates that when Sura
XXXVII speaks of God's 'announcement' of a son for Abraham it
could have referred only to Isaac, the son to be born to his elderly, and
supposedly barren, wife. The reason the announcement is repeated
after the intended sacrifice is to confirm that, having gone through the
experience, the son Isaac has become a Prophet. What confirms this
understanding is the fact that the passage in Sura XXXVII dealing with
the intended sacrifice ends (v. 113) with a blessing for Abraham and
Isaac. The absence of Ishmael's name here cannot be justified if he was
to have been the subject of the sacrifice.

At the time the Koran was first revealed to the world, the biblical
story about the sacrifice of Isaac was already known in Arabia through
the many Jewish tribes that had settled there. If the Koran had wanted
to contradict the biblical account, it would have stated the name
Ishmael clearly in this case. In fact, we have many sayings related to
Muhammad, through his uncle, Al-Abbas, confirming that the object
of the sacrifice was Isaac. Contrary to the belief of modern Islamic
scholars, the early Islamic scholar Al-Thaalabi emphasises expressly
that the Companions of the Prophet (Muhammad), such as Ali and

Omar, and their successors, agreed with the biblical story in this matter. Al-Thaalabi gives a similar account of the intended sacrifice to that we find in the Talmud: 'Taking a knife and rope they went together to the mount. Isaac said: "Father, take my shirt from my body, lest my dear mother find blood upon it and weep for me. Bind me firmly, so that I do not move, and look away while sacrificing me, lest you lose your courage."' Al-Kisa'i, another early Islamic scholar, even relates a rumour based on something we have already seen in the Talmud: 'When a rumour arose that Isaac was a foundling adopted by Abraham, God gave father and son the same figure, so that they were very like one another. But Abraham was grey.'

The reason why modern Muslim scholars have been prepared to go against all these views and insist that the sacrificed boy was Ishmael is the fact that they took the act to imply an honour for the victim, and they thought the Jews were trying to deprive their ancestor of an honour due to him. Yet to slaughter your own son as a sacrifice to the Lord was not the practice in Arabia, Mesopotamia or even Canaan at that time. Abraham's action can be explained only by the fact that he was trying to destroy a son who did not even look like him, who, according to the Talmud, 'all the people of the world suspected not to be his own son'—an heir to him who was, at the same time, an heir to the Pharaoh of Egypt.

Chapter 2

BIBLICAL SOURCES

Our standard translations of the Old Testament are based on the Massoretic Hebrew text, which goes back no further than the ninth or tenth centuries AD. This, in its turn, is said to have originated in the second century of the Christian era after a council had been convened at Jamnia, a small town near Jaffa, where Rabbi Johanan ben Zakki was allowed to live following the destruction of the Temple of Jerusalem by Titus's troops in AD 70. The Jewish authorities had become concerned that the Jews were using several versions of biblical books, especially after their dispersion, when the written Law became the only medium for Jewish unity. At Jamnia the form and content of the Old Testament were finally agreed upon, but the council made no textual changes, only choosing the books to be included in the Canon.

Hebrew, like other Semitic languages as well as hieroglyphs, does not have any written vowels and only the letters 'W' (*waw*) and 'Y' (*yodh*) can be used for 'U' and 'I'. Furthermore, the letter 'H' (*he*) can sometimes be read as a vowel (*A*) when placed at the end of a word. The question of true pronunciation, and thus interpretation of the sacred text, had therefore still to be settled. This was accomplished between the seventh and tenth centuries AD when a body of Jewish scholars took on the task of systemising the Massorah (tradition or measure) to formulate a standard pronunciation. Their work did not involve any change in the consonants, only the vowels, for which they adopted, shortly after the beginning of the tenth century, the Babylonian and Palestinian systems of placing the vowels above and between the consonants.

Yet the Hebrew Massoretic text is not the only Canon we have for the Old Testament. Older than it was the Greek text of Alexandria. How that version came into being is reported in a letter written by an unknown author about 100 BC: 'Ptolemy II, King of Egypt (285–247 BC), was persuaded by the Alexandrian librarian to have a Greek

translation made of the Bible. He appealed to the High Priest of
Jerusalem, who responded by sending seventy-two elders to Alexandria, six scholars from each of the twelve tribes of Israel, together with
an official copy of the Pentateuch (the first five books of the Old
Testament), written in letters of gold. They laboured for seventy-two
days to produce the final copy of the Pentateuch in Greek, which they
presented to the king.' Later the other books of the Old Testament
were also translated into Greek by other scholars and the whole work
became known as the Septuagint, which means 'The Seventy'. The
Greek text became the Bible of the Greek-speaking Jews, was widely
distributed throughout the Mediterranean world and was adopted as
the Bible of the early Church, only to be abandoned later in favour of
the Hebrew Massoretic text. Today, however, the Septuagint is still
used by the Greek Orthodox Church as its authorised Bible.

Flavius Josephus, the Jewish historian of priestly origin who was
born in AD 37, the year of the accession of Caligula in Rome, and who
wrote to the Greeks and Romans about his people's history and wars,
was the earliest, at the end of the first century AD, to designate the
books of the Old Testament as 'holy books'. For him the essential
characteristic of canonical Scripture was that it constituted pro-
nouncements of unquestioned authority that originated within the
prophetic period and were therefore divinely inspired. But when were
the inspired words of God first written down?

Ancient tradition attributed the authorship of the Pentateuch to
Moses, who is the divine instrument when writing is mentioned in the
Bible for the first time in the Book of Exodus: 'Then the Lord said to
Moses, "Write this on a scroll as something to be remembered and
make sure that Joshua hears it . . ."' Later we have the statement:
'Moses then wrote down everything the Lord had said', followed
shortly afterwards by yet a third reference to writing when the Law is
given to Moses on the top of Mount Sinai: 'The Lord said to Moses,
"Come up to me on the mountain and stay here, and I will give you the
tablets of stone, with the law and commands I have written for their
instruction".'

Although it seems that it was the Lord and not Moses who engraved
the words on stone on this occasion, there is no reason to doubt the
biblical statements that Moses was able to write. He would not have
written in either Hebrew or Aramaic because writing in those languages did not exist until the ninth or tenth centuries BC, but if Moses

had been brought up as an Egyptian prince—which is what he was—by the Pharaoh's daughter in the Royal palace, he is sure to have received instruction in the reading and writing of the Egyptian language.[1] Neither would he have learned to read and write Akkadian, the diplomatic language of the time, as R. K. Harrison, the Professor of Old Testament Studies at Toronto University, suggested in his book *Introduction to the Old Testament*. Why would an Egyptian prince learn the diplomatic language? This was the province of interpreters and scribes who communicated with foreigners, as we see from Joseph's story. It is also significant that Moses used the Egyptian method of writing—engraving on stone—while Akkadian cuneiform writing was usually done on clay. The Book of Deuteronomy also records that, at the time of the Exodus, Moses gave his followers instructions to erect a stele (an upright slab or pillar, usually with inscription and sculpture) in the Egyptian manner: '. . . Moses and the elders of Israel commanded the people, "Keep all these commands that I give you today. When you have crossed the Jordan into the land the Lord your God is giving you, set up some large stones and coat them with plaster. Write on them all the words of this law . . .".'

This means that the original biblical text written by Moses must have been in Egyptian. It was later used, together with some material transmitted orally, to compose the earliest written Hebrew texts around the ninth and eighth centuries BC, all of which have been lost. Against this background there were always those from the earliest days who questioned the historical worth of the Pentateuch. These critics pointed out the many contradictory versions within the same account, the mistakes in identifying historical characters and places, and the wider religious and mythological interpretations that make it difficult to accept much of the Old Testament version of events as

---

[1] A. S. Yahuda, the Hebrew and biblical scholar, points out in his book *The Language of the Pentateuch in its Relation to Egyptian*: 'In the Joseph and Exodus narratives there are expressions and turns of speech which are so unusual and appear so foreign that either their meaning is presumed merely from the context, as is usual in such cases, or they are taken by more modern interpreters as corruptions or mutilations.' He also goes on to say that the Hebrew narrator adapted Egyptian words and expressions into the Joseph story in Genesis verbatim: 'Even when Joseph speaks to his brothers, who as shepherds and Asiatics were regarded by the Egyptians as "barbarians", his words and expressions are cast in the superior tone of an Egyptian of high breeding, and the narrator very cleverly depicts how skilfully Joseph played the role of a genuine Egyptian before he revealed himself to his brothers.'

factual. As early as the first century of the Christian era it was questioned openly. In his treatise *Contra Apionem*, Flavius Josephus informs us that a number of Greek historians had disputed his earlier work, *The Antiquities of the Jews*, in which, he said, he had accurately described the contents of ancient Jewish records, 'neither adding anything to what is contained therein, nor taking away anything therefrom'. He noted also that there already existed a conflicting account of the Exodus that had been recorded by Manetho, the third-century Egyptian historian.

In Alexandria, which had become the centre of Greek culture and philosophy, it was Valentinus, the prominent Gnostic leader, who led the assault upon the text of the Old Testament in the second century AD, claiming that certain parts of the Pentateuch and the Prophets were not authentic, while the great Ptolemy, the astrologer and geographer of Italian origin, raised the basic question of the origin of the Pentateuch. In a letter containing his arguments, later found among the documents of the Greek writer Epiphanius, Ptolemy concluded that the five books of the Pentateuch attributed to Moses could not possibly have come from this single author, but must have been compiled by Moses from three sources—God, Moses himself and the Elders. However, with the acceptance of Christianity in AD 313 by Constantine the Great, who made it the official religion of the Roman Empire, and the decision of the Christian Council of Loadicia in 363 to include the Old Testament books (the Greek text) in the Christian Canon, belief in the divine inspiration and authorship of the Scriptures finally made the Bible the only acceptable historical source up to the end of the Middle Ages.

With the beginning of the Renaissance, when man decided to re-examine his previously accepted convictions in the light of the scientific rules he had discovered, powerful new voices were raised to challenge the belief that Moses wrote all the first five books of the existing text of the Pentateuch. Andreas Rudolf Bodestein, the German scholar (1480–1541), attacked the Mosaic authorship of the Pentateuch, basing his arguments on the fact that Moses could not possibly have written the account of his own death that occurs before the end of the Book of Deuteronomy: 'And Moses the servant of the Lord died there in Moab, as the Lord had said.' The English philosopher Thomas Hobbes (1588–1679) was another critic, taking the view that the writing of the Pentateuch took place long after Moses'

death. In his book *Tractatus Theologica-Politicus*, the Jewish philosopher Benedict Spinoza (1632–1677), who was a follower of
Hobbes, also entirely rejected the Mosaic authorship of the Pentateuch, insisting that the books from Genesis to Kings II were the work
of Ezra, the scribe and Hebrew scholar who lived during the fifth
century BC. A year after Spinoza's death came a further assault from
Richard Simon, the French priest and biblical critic, who declared in
his book *Histoire critique du Vieux Testament* that the Pentateuch was
the result of a long process of compilation and redaction of annals by a
guild of 'public scribes'. A few months after the book was published
the French Jansenists ordered it to be destroyed. In later years,
however, the work came to be regarded as the first attempt to treat the
Bible as a literary product.

Then came the turning point in the history of biblical criticism with
the ideas of Jean Astruc and their development by Old Testament
scholars, chiefly from Germany, in the first half of the nineteenth
century, followed by the work of Graf and Wellhausen, who regarded
the Pentateuch as essentially of composite origin, consisting of:

1   A Jehovistic source (J), dating from the ninth century BC.
2   An Elohistic document (E), dating from the eighth century BC.
3   The book of Deuteronomy (D), to be regarded as a separate
    source, dating from the seventh century BC.
4   A priestly source (P), dating from about the fifth century BC.
5   The work of an editor who revised and edited the entire collec-
    tion around the second century BC.

To apply this source analysis to the Joseph story:

THE DIVINE NAME

When we follow the documentary theorists in using the divine names
as a criterion for source analysis of the Joseph story, we find that
Elohim is used in eight chapters throughout the story, mainly in the
utterances of the characters, while Yahweh is used in only one chapter
(39). Thus the divine names alone are not enough to assist us in
dividing the Joseph story into (J) and (E) sources.

THE NAME OF JOSEPH'S FATHER

The father in the Joseph story is often referred to as 'their father' when
the brothers are mentioned or 'his father' in the case of Joseph. In other

cases he is referred to by name. Jacob, his original name, and Israel, the new one given to him by the Lord, alternate throughout the story, each appearing in fifteen verses.[1] This alternation of the father's names has been accepted as two parallel documentary sources behind the Joseph story.

THE NAME OF THE GOOD BROTHER

The names of Judah and Reuben also alternate in the role of the 'good brother' who tries to protect Joseph, counselling the other brothers not to kill him. The names Judah and Reuben also coincide with the occurrence of the names Israel and Jacob respectively. This alternation in the good brother's name has also been accepted as a valid criterion for source analysis. When we apply these criteria to the Joseph story, we come to the following conclusions:[2]

Ch. 37: This chapter, which introduces the plot of the Joseph story, is a combination of the Judah-Israel version (J) and the Reuben-Jacob version (E).

Ch. 38, interrupting the story of Joseph to report the events that took place in Canaan between Judah and Tamar, his daughter-in-law, belongs to (J).

Ch. 39, concerning Joseph in Potiphar's house and the relationship with his master's wife, belongs almost completely to (J).

Ch. 40: Joseph in prison, where he interprets the dreams of the cupbearer and the baker; vv. 1, 15b come from (J) and vv. 2–15a, 16–23, from (E).

Ch. 41: This chapter, dealing with Joseph's audience with Pharaoh, his appointment as vizier, his Egyptian name and Egyptian wife, and the birth of his two sons, belongs to (E) except for v. 46, giving Joseph's age as thirty at the time, which is a priestly insertion (P).

Ch. 42: vv. 1–4, Joseph sending his sons, except Benjamin, to Egypt is (E); vv. 5–7, where Joseph meets his brothers, is (J); vv. 8–37, with the accusation of spying, then allowing the brothers to leave with Simeon, is (E); v. 38, the last of the chapter, in which the father refuses

---

[1] Jacob appears in ch. 37, vv. 1, 2, 34; ch. 42, vv. 1, 4, 29, 36; ch. 43, v. 2; ch. 45, vv. 25, 27; ch. 47, vv. 7, 8, 9, 10, 28; Israel appears in ch. 37, vv. 3, 13, 14; ch. 42, v. 5; ch. 43, vv. 6, 8, 11; ch. 45, vv. 21, 28; ch. 46, vv. 29, 30; ch. 47, vv. 27, 29, 31; ch. 50, v. 2.

[2] *Introduction à l'ancien Testament*, L. Gautier; and *Joseph en Egypte*, Joseph Vergote.

Reuben's request to let Benjamin go with the brothers to Egypt, is (J).
Ch. 43: The account of the brothers' second visit to Egypt and their lunch at Joseph's house belongs to (J) apart from v. 14a (P) and v. 14b, c (E).
Ch. 44: The accusation against Benjamin, in order to keep him in Egypt, that he has stolen Joseph's cup comes from (J).
Ch. 45: Here Joseph reveals himself to his brothers and asks them to bring their father and families to live in Egypt; vv. 1–15 are from (J), vv. 16–28 from (E).
Ch. 46: The Israelites' descent into Egypt; vv. 1a, 28–34 are (J); vv. 1b–5 are (E); vv. 6–8a are (P), also vv. 26–27 giving the number of Israel's family that went down to Egypt.
Ch. 47: Most of this chapter, dealing with the settlement in Goshen and the agrarian reforms, comes from (J), with the exception of Jacob's audience with Pharaoh (vv. 5–11) and the length of Israel's stay in Egypt (vv. 27–28), which belong to (P).
Ch. 48: Jacob's sickness (vv. 1–3a) comes from (E); God's promise to Jacob (vv. 3b–4) and Rachel's burial in Bethlehem (v. 7) come from (P); Israel's blessing of Joseph's sons, Manasseh and Ephraim, belongs to (J).
Ch. 49: vv. 1–28, which make up the narration known as 'The Benediction of Jacob' and contain Jacob's blessing for the twelve sons of Israel, contain elements of both (J) and (E) and are thought to be the work of the editor; the rest of the chapter, dealing with his request to be buried in Canaan and his death, is another priestly addition (P).
Ch. 50: The embalming of Jacob and the burial journey to Canaan have (J) as their source; vv. 12–13, relating the sons' burial of their father in Abraham's cave, come from (P); the rest of the chapter, concerning Joseph's death, is from (E).[1]

---

[1] Joseph Vergote, in *Joseph en Egypte*, assigns this section to (J).

Chapter 3

WHO WAS TUYA?

There is an Egyptian tradition, later included in the Islamic traditions from which it passed into Jewish literature,[1] that the name of Potiphar's wife was Zelekha. This name is absent from both biblical and koranic narrations, but the Egyptian tradition indicates that it was she who was given to Joseph in marriage.

One of Tuya's titles is *kheret nesw*, which, according to Alan Gardiner[2] and T. G. H. James,[3] means 'the king's ornament'. Arthur Weigall thought that she might have been a member of the Royal family. He comments in *The Life and Times of Akhnaten*: 'She . . . may have been, for instance, the grand-daughter of Tuthmosis III, to whom she bears some likeness in face. Queen Tiye is often called "Royal Daughter" as well as "Royal Wife", and it is possible that this is to be taken literally.' He goes on to remark that, after her daughter's marriage to Amenhotep III, 'Tuya . . . included among her titles "Royal Handmaid" (or lady-in-waiting), "the favoured one of Hathor", "the favourite of the king",[4] a title which may indicate that she was of Royal blood.' He also thinks the fact that she and Yuya were given a fine large tomb in the Valley of the Kings makes this more likely.

---

[1] Sefer ha-Yashar, *The Haggadah*.

[2] *Egyptian Grammar*.

[3] *Corpus of Hieroglyphic Inscriptions in the Brooklyn Museum*.

[4] Three different forms of this title were found in Yuya's tomb: a) *ḥsyt nt ntr nfr*—favoured of the good god (the king); b) *ḥsyt nt Ḥr m pr-f*—favoured of Horus in his house (the king in his palace); c) *ḥsyt nt Ḥr nb t3 pn*—favoured of Horus, Lord of this land (the king).

Chapter 4

JOSEPH'S NAME

The German scholar Georg Steindorff[1] was the first to identify an Egyptian original of the Hebrew name, Zaphnath-pa-a-neah, that Pharaoh gave to Joseph on appointing him as his vizier. As both Hebrew and ancient Egyptian had no written short vowels, he identified the consonants as follows:

Z	ph	nth	ph	'nh
ḏd	p3	nṯr	iw-f	'nḫ
says (speaks)	the	god	is-he	live

'The god speaks: may he live', or: 'God says he will live'.

From the phonetic standpoint, this reading was thought possible, and such names were found frequently among Egyptians. However, Abraham S. Yahuda[2] showed later that there are two arguments against such a reading: names of this kind were not found before the Twenty-first Dynasty (1087 BC into the closing centuries of the first millenium BC), and they always include a divine name—Amun, Horus, Isis, Min and so on—where Steindorff read 'the God'. He also argued that Pharaoh must have bestowed on Joseph a name that was meaningful in the context of the story, a name appropriate to his role as saviour of the land. Yahuda, who believed that Joseph's descent into Egypt must have taken place at a much earlier time than the Twentieth Dynasty, therefore suggested an alternative reading:

Z-ph	n	th	ph	'nh
ḏf3	n	t3	p3	'nḫ
food (sustenance)	of	land	the	life

---

[1] 'Der Name Josephs Saphenal-Pa'neach', *Zeitschrift für Ägyptische Sprache*, vol. 27, 1889.
[2] *The Language of the Pentateuch in its Relation to Egyptian.*

This he translated as: 'Food, sustenance of the land, is living.' Not only does this interpretation relate Joseph to his right biblical role: Yahuda was able to show by many examples that *df 3* (food) was used in names from the time of the Middle Kingdom, about a millennium before the interpretation offered by Steindorff and even before the Hyksos invasion. Later still, however, Joseph Vergote showed in *Joseph en Egypte* that Yahuda's identification, too, was not possible. For in Yahuda's reading, the *p3* before the final *'nh* is regarded as the article 'the', in which case *t3* (land) should also have been preceded by the article.

Vergote, using the Greek version of the name in the text of Flavius Josephus, gave his own interpretation:

$$p3 \quad s \quad nty \quad 'm\text{-}f \quad n3 \quad ih(t)$$

This would mean 'the man who knows things' and derives from a title of the magicians, *Khartumim (rh-ih-t)*, which means literally 'he who knows the things', the name given as a paraphrase of the old title in the spoken language of the period. This language, called Late Egyptian, was also employed in non-literary documents during the early Eighteenth Dynasty, even before the time of Tuthmosis III. Then, during the time of Yuya's grandson, Akhnaten, it was used in addition in works of literature. By giving this name to Joseph, Vergote claimed, Pharaoh was hitting back at the pretentious persons who had not been able to interpret his dreams.

Many others scholars have also attempted to present different readings of the biblical name and find the original Egyptian, but none has yet produced a form that has gained general acceptance. This, in my view, has resulted from misreading of the first element in the biblical name and its Egyptian equivalent. If we look back to Steindorff's reading, we find that he transliterated the initial Z into an Egyptian *dd*. The fact that this was accepted by the rest of the scholars has caused all the misinterpretations that have followed.

It is true that an Egyptian *d* (the letter *dad*, pronounced as in 'dump') is transliterated into Hebrew as Z (the Hebrew letter *sadhe*, pronounced as the 's' in 'sun') because Hebrew does not have a similar letter. This process cannot take place in reverse, however, because Egyptian has separate sounds for Z and D. To repeat an earlier example, B and V have the same sound in Spanish but different sounds in English.

Hebrew has four letters giving an S sound: *zayin (Z)*, *sámekh (S)*, *ṣadhe (Ṣ)* and *śin (Ś)*. Although all the sounds produced by the four Hebrew letters did exist in the ancient Egyptian language, they were originally written with one letter, S—although it was represented by more than one sign—which was the Egyptian equivalent of the Hebrew *sámekh*. If we read the name given to Joseph in the light of this, we have:

Z   ph   nth   ph   'nh
S   ph   nṯr   iw-f   'nh

In fact, the first two elements (*S-ph*) or Seph form the second part of Joseph's name and make up the Egyptian *Sp*, common among personal Egyptian names, both masculine and feminine, during the Old, Middle and New Kingdoms, where we find the following examples:

Sp, Sp-wr.t, Sp-n, Sp-n-wrdt.t, Sp-n.mw-t, Sp-nfr, Sp-y, Sp-s.[1]

Sp or Seph had many meanings in Egyptian—time, matter (affair, case), deed (act, creation), misdeed (fault), occasion (chance), venture, success, condition, medicine (dose), portion of food and others. There are therefore a large variety of interpretations possible for Joseph's Egyptian name: 'The creation of god, let him live' . . . 'The success of god' . . . 'The medicine of god'. The name does not help to relate him to any specific period of Egyptian history, but it does confirm that the biblical name was not just a late colouring on the part of the biblical narrator, but was an authentic Egyptian name that related both to history and the Bible.

[1] *Die Ägyptische Personennamen*, Hermann Ranke.

BIBLIOGRAPHY

ALBRIGHT, WILLIAM, *The Archaeology of Palestine*, London, 1963.

BAKIR, ABD EL-MOHSEN, *Slavery in Pharaonic Egypt*. Supplement to *Annales du Service des Antiquités de l'Egypte*, Cairo, vol. 18, 1952.

BREASTED, JOHN H., *A History of Egypt*, Chicago, 1921.

—— *Ancient Records of Egypt*, vol. 2, Chicago, 1906.

BROWN, F., DRIVER, S. R., BRIDGES, C. A., *A Hebrew and English Lexicon of the Old Testament*, Oxford, 1907.

CONDER, C. R., *The Tell Amarna Tablets*, London, 1893.

DASSAUD, R. H. R., *Les Découvertes des Ras Shamra et l'ancien Testament*, 1941.

DAVIES, N. DE G., 'The Tombs of Djehuty and Antef' in *Studies in Honour of F. Ll Griffith*, London, 1932.

DAVIS, THEODORE M., *The Tomb of Iouiya and Touiyou*, London, 1907.

DESROCHES-NOBLECOURT, CHRISTINE, *Tutankhamen*, London, 1963.

DRIOTON, ETIENNE, 'Un Document sur la vie chère à Thèbes au début de la XVIII dynastie' in the *Bulletin of the Société Française d'Egypte*, Cairo.

FAULKNER, R. O. D., *A Concise Dictionary of Middle Egyptian*, Oxford, 1964.

GARDINER, ALAN, *Egypt of the Pharaohs*, Oxford, 1961.

—— 'A New Rendering of Egyptian Texts' in *The Journal of Egyptian Archaeology*, London, vol. 5, 1918.

—— *Egyptian Grammar*, Oxford, 1950.

—— *The Tomb of Amenemhet*, London, 1915.

GAUTIER, LUCIEN, *Introduction à l'ancien Testament*, Paris, 1916.

GORDON, CYRUS H., *The World of the Old Testament*, 1960.

—— *Ugaritic Manual*, III, 1955.

GUNN, B., and GARDINER, ALAN, in *The Journal of Egyptian Archaeology*, London, vol. 5, 1918.

HABACHI, LABIB, *Annales du Service des Antiquités de l'Egypte*, Cairo, vol. 53, 1956.

HARRISON, R. K., *Introduction to the Old Testament*, London, 1970.

JAMES, T. G. H., *Corpus of Hieroglyphic Inscriptions in the Brooklyn Museum*.

JOSEPHUS, FLAVIUS, *Contra Apionem*, translated by H. St. J. Thackeray, London and New York, 1926.

KALISCH, M. M., *A Historical and Critical Commentary on the Old Testament*, London, 1858.

KITCHEN, K. A., *Ancient Orient and the Old Testament*, Illinois, 1966.

LAMBDIN, T. O., *Egyptian Loan Words and Transcriptions in the Ancient Semitic Languages*, Baltimore, 1952.

MASPERO, GASTON, *The Struggle of the Nations*, London, 1896.

NAVILLE, H. E., *Funerary Papyrus of Iouiya*, London, 1908.

PEET, T. E., *Egypt and the Old Testament*, London, 1922.

PETRIE, W. M. FLINDERS, *Hyksos and Israelite Cities*, London, 1906.

—— *A History of Egypt*, II, London, 1894.

POLANO, H., *Selections from the Talmud*, London, 1894.

PORTER, BERTHA, and MOSS, ROSALIND, *Topographical Bibliography of Ancient Hieroglyphic Texts, Reliefs and Paintings*, Oxford, 1964.

PRITCHARD, J. B., *Ancient Near Eastern Texts*, Princeton, 1955.

QUIBELL, JAMES E., *Catalogue général des antiquités égyptiennes du Musée du Caire, Tomb of Yuaa and Thuiu*, Cairo, 1908.

RANKE, HERMANN, *Die Agyptischen Personennamen*, Munich, 1902.

REDFORD, DONALD B., *A Study of the Biblical Story of Joseph*, Leiden, 1970.

ROWLEY, H. H., *From Joseph to Joshua*, London, 1950.

SCHULMAN, A. R., in *Journal of the American Research Centre in Egypt*, Cairo, vol. 2, 1963.

SETHE, KURT, *Das Ägyptische Verbum*, Leipzig, 1899–1902.

SIMON, RICHARD, *Histoire critique du Vieux Testament*, 1678.

SPINOZA, BENEDICT, *Tractatus Theologica-Politicus*.

STEINDORFF, G., 'Der Name Josephs Saphenal-Pa neach' in *Zeitschrift für Ägyptische Sprache*, Leipzig, vol. 27, 1889.

VAN SETERS, JOHN, *The Hyksos*, New Haven and London, 1966.

VERGOTE, JOSEPH, *Joseph en Egypte*, Louvain, 1959.

WEIGALL, ARTHUR, *The Life and Times of Akhnaten*, London, 1910 and 1923.

WILSON, J. A., 'The Oath in Ancient Egypt' in *Journal of Near Eastern Studies*, vol. 7, 1948.

YAHUDA, A. S., *The Language of the Pentateuch in its Relation to Egyptian*, Oxford, 1933.

'Prices and Wages in Egypt in the Ramesside Period' in *Cahiers d'histoire mondiale*, Part I, vol. 4, 1954.

Zeitschrift für Ägyptische Sprache, vol. 15, 1887.

────── vol. 39, 1901.

INDEX

Aaron 119, 147
Abraham (Abram) 32–7, 39, 41,
    53–4, 114–15, 117–18, 120,
    134, 145–8, 150–2, 159
Abu Bakr 54
Ahmose 80, 85, 109, 130
Ahmosis I 78–80, 96, 109, 120, 131
Akhetaten (city) 138–9
Akhnaten see Amenhotep IV
Al-Abbas 151
Alalakh VII 81–2
Albright, W. 75, 81, 164
Aldred, C. 132
Alexander the Great 71
Al-Kisa'i 152
Al-Thaalabi 151–2
Amarna
    kings 87, 91, 128, 137–9, 142
    tablets 35–6, 139
Amenemhet III 84
Amenemhet (son of Tuthmosis IV)
    66
Amenhotep
    I 79–80
    II 93, 95
    III 14, 21, 24, 28, 36, 39, 63–8,
        83, 97, 118, 121–3, 126, 129,
        138–40, 160
    IV (Akhnaten) 14, 28, 63, 65, 68,
        86–7, 118, 120, 123, 137–9,
        162
Amenipet 66

Amun (Egyptian god) 138, 161
Amurrites 73, 81–2
Anen (son of Yuya) 97, 129, 132
Ankhsenpaaten 138
Apachmen 70
Apophis 70, 77, 82, 89, 92
Asenath (Joseph's wife) 48, 85,
    90–3, 125–6
Assis 70
Astruc, J. 29, 157
Aten (Egyptian god) 123, 137–8
Avaris 71, 76, 78–9, 92, 96, 101,
    107–12, 118, 139
Aye (son of Yuya) 14, 63, 102, 118,
    125, 132, 137–8
Ayrton, E. 21

Bakir, A. 85, 94–5, 164
Belzoni, G. 101–2
Benjamin 49–50, 55, 59, 94, 96,
    158–9
ben Zakki, J. 153
Bible and biblical studies 29–43, 54,
    60–1, 69, 75, 84–6, 90, 93,
    112, 114–116, 118, 130,
    135–6, 141–2, 145, 151,
    153–60
Bilhah 42, 131
Bnon 70
Bodestein, A. R. 156
Breasted, J. H. 64, 111, 127, 164
Brugsch, E. 107

Cairo 18, 67, 86, 103, 109
Canaan 34–5, 42, 48–53, 81, 90
Carnarvon
    Lord 76
    Tablet 89
Carter, H. 21
Champollion, J. F. 101–2
chariots 75–83, 127–8
circumcision 35
Constantine the Great 156
Copts 98, 102

Dassaud, R. H. R. 90, 164
Davis, T. M. 17, 21–3, 26, 66–7,
    99, 141, 164
Dead Sea Scrolls 31
Descent into Egypt 30, 52, 115,
    117, 131, 161 see also Joseph
Desroches-Noblecourt, C. 67, 164

Egypt 13–18, 21–28, 30, 33–52,
    58–60, 62, 69–77, 83–142
    cities of see specific names e.g.
        Cairo, Memphis
    gods of see specific names e.g.
        Osiris
Egypt Exploration Society (Fund)
    17, 103, 143
Elliot Smith, G. see Smith, G. E.
Ephraim (Joseph's son) 48, 52–3,
    125, 130, 159
Esau 39, 41–2, 44, 118, 120, 148
Exodus, Book of 29, 86, 100,
    106–7, 116–19, 135, 154–5
Exodus, The 13–15, 17–18, 30,
    53–4, 60, 69–71, 73, 100–1,
    103, 106–18, 126, 135–6,
    141–2, 155–6
Ezra 30, 157

Faqus 107–8
Flinders Petrie, W. M. 21, 99, 103,
    165

Gardiner, A. 73, 77, 81, 89, 92, 99,
    106, 108, 110, 118, 129, 132,
    160, 164
Gautier, L. 158, 164
Genesis, Book of 29, 32, 33, 44–5,
    53, 61, 75, 84–6, 88–90,
    94–5, 97–8, 107, 115–16,
    121–2, 127–31, 133–4
Goodwin, C. W. 133
Gordon, C. H. 90, 115, 117, 164
Goshen 51, 69, 74–5, 100–1, 107,
    109, 112–13, 118, 129
Graf, K. H. 29–30

Habachi, L. 108, 165
Hagar 36, 54, 145
Harrison, R. K. 155, 165
Hatshepsut 21, 63, 92, 120
Hebrews see Israel, tribe of
Herodotus 98
Hittites 81
Hobbes, T. 156–7
Horemheb 15, 63, 87, 111–12, 118,
    120, 137–9
Hurrians 39, 76, 81
Hyksos Kings of Egypt 13, 16, 26,
    69–71, 73–82, 84, 87, 89,
    91–101, 112, 114, 118, 162

Isaac 36–9, 41, 53, 118, 120–1,
    123, 134, 145–8, 150–2
Ishmael 36, 41, 54, 145, 147–8,
    151–2
Islam see Koran
Israel, tribe of 13, 36, 44, 47, 50,
    55, 62, 69, 71, 73–4, 90, 97,
    99–101, 105–6, 112–13, 126,
    131, 134, 141–2, 159 see also
    Jacob, Joseph

Jacob 30–1, 38–44, 48, 51–3, 55,
    59–60, 62, 98–9, 114–15,

117–18, 120, 123, 130–2,
  134–5, 147–8, 150
James, T. G. H. 141, 160, 165
Jamnia 153
Janna 70
Janssen, J. M. 133
Jesus 32, 38, 54, 98, 142, 148–9
Joseph (Yussuf) 13–14, 16–18, 26,
  29–61, 69–71, 74–6, 81–100,
  103, 109, 111, 114, 116–18,
  120–3, 125–36, 139, 141,
  147, 155, 157–9, 161–3
  name 48, 90–1, 121, 157, 161–3
  positions 127
  wife 48, 85, 90–3 *see also*
  Asenath
Josephus, F. 70–1, 73, 107, 109,
  126, 154, 156, 162, 165
Joshua 135, 154
Judah 30–1, 45, 50, 53, 158

Kalisch, M. M. 114, 165
Kamose 76–8, 82
  Stele 89, 109
Karnak 102
Keturah 36
Kirgipa 64
Kitchen, K. A. 115, 165
Koran 15, 54–61, 69–70, 84, 93,
  96, 141, 145–52, 160
Kuthman, C. 111

Leah 42, 131
Lefebvre, G. 133
Lepsius, K. 102–3, 105
Levi 115–17
Loadicia, Council of 156
Lot 33

Makir 53
Manasseh (Joseph's son) 48, 52–3,
  116, 130, 159

Manetho 70–1, 73, 92, 96, 109,
  126, 156
Mariette, F. 102–3, 112
Maspero, G. 23, 26, 62, 64, 67,
  123, 125, 165
Memphis 34, 109–10, 113, 138
Menes 71
Merenptah 103
Misphrag-mouthosis 71
monotheism 28, 123, 137–9, 142
Montet, P. 108
Moses 13, 15, 17–18, 29, 54–5, 60,
  70–1, 100–1, 113, 116–17,
  119, 135–6, 142, 147, 154–7
Moss, R. 97, 165
Muhammad 54, 151
mummification 15, 98–9, 140–1, 159
Mutnedjemet 139

Naville, H. 18, 26, 103, 105–8,
  125, 128, 133, 165
Nebaioth 41
Nefertiti 132, 138
Newberry, P. E. 132
Nuzi tablets 39

On (Heliopolis) 34, 107
  priest of 48, 85–6, 92–3, 129
Osarseph 71
Osiris (Egyptian god) 92, 98, 126,
  137, 142

Papyrus Anastasi 110–11
Papyrus Sallier I 92
Peet, E. 70, 74, 92, 165
Pepi 77
Pharaoh 13–14, 34–7, 43, 46–9,
  51–3, 58, 62, 69–70, 75, 81,
  84–5, 88, 90, 93, 97, 100,
  102–3, 106, 112, 118–20,
  126–32, 134, 145, 152, 155,
  158–9, 161–2

Pi-Ramses 101, 105, 107–10, 112–13, 117–18
Pi-thom 101, 103, 105–7, 118
Polano, H. 42, 130
Porter, B. 97, 165
Potiphar 45–6, 56–8, 84–6, 120, 158, 160
Potipherah 48, 85, 90
Pritchard, J. B. 92, 165
Ptolemy of Alexandria 107, 153–4, 156

Qantir 108
Quibell, J. 21–2, 25, 66–7, 123–4, 128, 165

Ra (Egyptian god) 92–3, 105, 112, 137
Rachel 42, 49, 55, 131, 159
Ramses 82, 139
  I 15, 118–19
  II 69, 73, 77, 100, 102, 105–6, 108–13, 118
  III 21–4, 109
  XI 21–3
Ranke, H. 91, 163, 165
Rebekah 38–9, 121
Redford, D. B. 30, 60, 84, 86, 89, 91, 134–5, 165
Restoration stele 138
Reuben 30–1, 45, 94, 158–9
Rosetta stone 101
Rossellini 65
Rowley, H. H. 117

Sadat, A. 140–1
Saleh, M. 140–1
Salitis 70
Salt, H. 102
Sarah (Sarai) (wife of Abraham) 33–9, 41, 54, 117–18, 121, 145, 150–1

Schulman, A. R. 82, 165
Sefer ha-Yashar 160
Sekenen-re 79
Semenkhkare 14, 63, 118, 120, 137–9
Seth (Egyptian god) 92, 98, 109, 111–12, 137, 142
Sethe, K. 91, 165
Seti I 102, 109, 112, 118, 139
Simeon 49, 158
Simon, R. 157, 165
Sinuhe 88
Sitamun 14, 63, 65–8
slavery in Egypt 84–5, 100–1
Smith, G. Elliot 67, 124–5, 133
sojourn in Egypt 14–15, 17
Spiegelberg, W. 91
Spinoza, B. 157, 165
Steindorff, G. 111, 161–2, 165
Succoth 106–7, 117
Suez Canal 105

Tanis 102, 108, 111
Tarkhun Dara 36
Tell el-Maskhuta see Succoth
Tentamun 66
Terah 32–3
Teti 77
Tey (wife of Aye) 132
Thebes 96, 102–3, 111, 113, 118, 132, 138
Thoumosis 71
Tia 66
Tiye (daughter of Yuya) 28, 39, 63–8, 111, 118, 121, 123, 131–2, 137, 140, 160
Tum Harmakhis (Egyptian god) 62, 105–6
Tutankhamun 14, 16, 25–6, 63, 102, 113, 118, 125–6, 132, 137–9

Tuthmosis
  I 80, 112
  III 82, 85, 87, 109, 118, 120, 122,
    160, 162
  IV 14, 21, 62–3, 66, 68, 93,
    117–18, 120, 123, 128–9, 137
Tutimaios 70
Tuya (wife of Yuya) 21, 23–4,
    26–8, 63–4, 67–8, 91, 125–6,
    129, 131–2, 160

Uthman 54

Valentinus 156
Valley of Nobles 26
Valley of the Kings 21, 160
Van Seters, J. 81, 165
Vergote, J. 87, 89, 91, 97, 158–9,
    162, 165

Weigall, A. 21–2, 25, 27, 67, 160,
    166
Wellhausen, J. 30, 157

Yahuda, A. S. 87–8, 127, 155,
    161–2, 166
Yuya 15–18, 22–8, 62–8, 82–3,
    86, 91, 117, 120–9, 131–3,
    137–41, 160, 162
  origin 124–6
  spelling of name 121–4
  titles of 26–7
  tomb of 15–17, 21, 23–5, 140
  wife of see Tuya

Zaru 109–12, 118
Zelekha 160
Zilpah 42, 131
Zoan 107–8